ALFRED CHESTER BEATTY
AND IRELAND 1950-1968
A Study in Cultural Politics

Alfred Chester Beatty
and Ireland 1950-1968
A Study in Cultural Politics

Brian P Kennedy

THE GLENDALE PRESS

First published 1988 by
The Glendale Press
18 Sharavogue
Glenageary Rd. Upper
Dun Laoghaire
Co. Dublin
Ireland

ISBN 0 907606 49 0

Cover by Q Design
Typeset by Wendy A. Commins, The Curragh
Make-up by Paul Bray
Printed in Great Britain by,
Richard Clay Ltd, Bungay, Suffolk

In memory of Donal McLoughlin

Contents

Plates

Acknowledgements

This work would not have been possible without the co-operation of the Trustees of the Chester Beatty Library. I would also like to record my thanks to the Librarian, Mr Wilfrid Lockwood, and to each member of the staff for invaluable help and encouragement.

I wish to express my gratitude to Mr Ted Nealon, T.D., former Minister of State for Arts and Culture, for permission to consult records held by the Department of the Taoiseach; to Mr Richard Stokes, Assistant Secretary, Department of the Taoiseach; to Mr Sean Donlon, former Secretary, Department of Foreign Affairs, for permission to consult files held by that Department; to Ms Anne Neary of the State Paper Office, and Mr David Craig of the Public Record Office; to Ms Ann Stewart and Ms Catherine deCourcey of the National Gallery of Ireland; to Ms K. Janet Wallace of the British Museum and Mr Stephen Calloway of the Victoria and Albert Museum; and to Ms Cindy Smith and Mr Cyril Kidd, formerly of Selection Trust Limited.

It is a great pleasure to acknowledge the assistance of the staffs of the libraries of University College, Dublin, the National Library of Ireland, and Trinity College, Dublin. I am very grateful to all those who agreed to be interviewed. Where possible, reference has been made to them and to others who assisted me by acknowledgements in the footnotes. I wish to thank Mrs Betty Geraghty who typed the final manuscript.

I owe five special debts — to the Authorities of University College, Dublin, for providing me with a scholarship to pursue this research; to the National University of Ireland for a grant-in-aid of publication; to Professor Kevin B. Nowlan, for his keen interest, excellent advice and warm good nature at all stages in the preparation of this study; to the Royal Irish Academy for awarding me the Edmund Curtis Memorial Prize, 1986; and to my family and friends for patiently listening to more about Chester Beatty than they probably deserved to hear.

Abbreviations

CBP	Chester Beatty Papers; Chester Beatty Library, Dublin.
D/Ex A	Department of External Affairs; files held by the Irish Department of Foreign Affairs, Iveagh House, Dublin.
H.C.Deb.	Parliamentary Debates of the House of Commons, Westminster.
NGI CB	National Gallery of Ireland, Dublin; Chester Beatty files.
SPO	State Paper Office; Dublin Castle.
TCD	Trinity College, Dublin.
UCD A	University College, Dublin, Archives Department.

Introduction

It is not often that Irish politicians and civil servants are congratulated for their attitudes and responses regarding cultural policy. There are many instances of delay and neglect, puritanism and censorship, hypocrisy and token gestures. The case of Alfred Chester Beatty and Ireland is, however, singularly enlightening.

The Irish Government's reaction to the arrival of a wealthy Irish-American mining magnate who wished to make Dublin the home of his private collection of Oriental art and manuscripts provides an interesting example of the interplay of cultural politics.

Beatty was no ordinary visitor to Ireland. At a time of mass-emigration he declared his belief in the future of the country, and as proof of his sincerity offered many gifts to the Irish nation. In return he hoped to be treated with special consideration. The Irish Government responded by making him the most honoured cultural benefactor in the country's history.

This study is intended as a modest contribution to near-contemporary Irish cultural history. There is much work to be done in this area which has been largely neglected, perhaps due to an over-preoccupation by scholars with purely political history.

Chapter 1

A Study in Cultural Politics

*Our first need in Ireland, if we had realised it, was not
a political republic but a cultural republic. We made a
mistake. We have to rectify it.*

Thomas McGreevy

The fervour of Irish cultural life in the period leading to the
birth of the Irish Free State was sadly not reflected in official
attitudes to culture after 1922. The Second Dáil (26 August
1921 – 9 January 1922) saw fit to appoint a Minister for Fine
Arts but no Irish Government created a similar Ministry for
another sixty years.

The Arts were not on the priority list at the foundation of
the State. This situation is certainly understandable in a
newly independent nation grappling with the problems of
providing an infrastructure – roads, electricity, housing,
drainage, transport, schools and hospitals. But although not a
top priority at any time, cultural policy after independence
was condemned to a narrow interpretation which involved a
determined rejection of all that was associated with the
previous eight centuries of oppression. Thus it was that the
policy of an Irish Ireland became official, based on two major
planks – the Catholic religion and the Irish language.[1] It
encouraged an atmosphere of intolerance, puritanism and
censorship.

Much has been written of the tragedy and paucity of
intellectual and cultural life in Ireland from 1922 to 1950.
It is unfortunate that this writing has not been more generous

as it has directed our attention away from another reality. Why did a man like Alfred Chester Beatty choose to live in a country of which it has been said:

> An attitude of xenophobic suspicion often greeted any manifestation of what appeared to reflect cosmopolitan standards. An almost Stalinist antagonism to modernism, to surrealism, free verse, symbolism and the modern cinema was combined with prudery . . . and a deep reverence for the Irish past.[2]

Thomas Bodkin wrote in 1949, the year Beatty decided to move to Ireland:

> We have not merely failed to go forward in policies concerning the Arts, we have, in fact, regressed to arrive, many years ago, at a condition of apathy about them in which it had become justifiable to say of Ireland that no country of Western Europe cared less, or gave less, for the cultivation of the Arts.[3]

Beatty read Bodkin's remarks but they did not deter him. Why not? The reason is simple — Beatty found Ireland to be a country with charm and atmosphere. He liked the people and once this was established in his mind he was prepared to allow cultural policies to take care of themselves. He was conservative in his personal life and approved of the general sentiment as expressed by Eamon de Valera:

> The Irish genius has always stressed spiritual and intellectual rather than material values. That is the characteristic that fits the Irish people in a special manner for the task, now a vital one, of helping to save Western civilisation.[4]

This cultural view was shared by many of de Valera's political opponents.[5] The Irish destiny in this world was other-worldly, that is, spiritual. The very first editorial which appeared in the *Irish Press* reflects de Valera's views (and indeed may have been written by him):

> Our ideal culturally is an Irish Ireland aware of its own greatness, sure of itself, conscious of the spiritual forces which have formed it into a distinct people having its

16

own language and customs and a traditionally Christian philosophy of life.[6]

The other reality which has hitherto been neglected is the cultural life which *was* present in the period from 1922 to 1950. Beatty described Dublin as 'a city of wonderful culture and art consciousness'.[7] Was he being diplomatic or suffering from self-delusion? Neither is true because, in fact, there was a vibrant cultural life in Dublin founded on what one might call culture with a small 'c', that of localised, community-based, familial involvement in activities ranging from drama groups to dancing classes, religious organisations to charitable societies, book clubs to 'feiseanna'. Beatty may have concentrated his efforts early in life on 'material values' but in retirement he came to appreciate 'spiritual and intellectual values' and 'Christian philosophy'. He considered that this was the most important factor in Irish cultural life.

Nevertheless, official attitudes to the visual arts were stunted. Bodkin wrote of a 'neglect, amounting almost to contempt for Art in our educational system'.[8] It was seen as a luxury and there were many more pressing concerns. De Valera frankly admitted that he knew little or nothing about art.[9] He was, however, a shrewd politician, an opportunist who courted Beatty because of the prestige attached to his name and that of his collections.

Beatty offered so much that he could not be refused. His reception in Ireland was facilitated by his personal friendship with political leaders. Disinterested in Irish party politics, Beatty came to know men like Eamon de Valera and Seán T. O'Kelly by discussing cultural matters. While the general public saw de Valera as an austere statesman, Beatty knew him as a friend and described him as 'such a nice man — so thoughtful and considerate — and also he is a great man — so simple and unassuming'.[10]

The special treatment which Beatty was to receive in Ireland achieves its proper perspective when it is compared with the treatment accorded some other cultural matters in the same period. For example, the Abbey Theatre, which burned down in 1951, was not rebuilt until 1966. Thomas McGreevy, Director of the National Gallery of Ireland (1950-64), applied for funds to build an extension in 1951 but the money was not offered until 1962. Public interest was excited in 1961 when it was revealed that a site had been purchased for a new National Library. Twenty-five years later the plans have still not been realised.

A list of reports and inquiries of the Irish Dáil and Senate in the period from 1922 to 1972 reveals thirty-four reports under the heading 'National Culture'.[11] If this figure is broken down the position of the visual arts becomes apparent — The Gaeltacht (14 Reports), The Irish Language (7), Historical Manuscripts and the Arts (6), Broadcasting and Television (5), Population (2). Of the six reports on Historical Manuscripts and the Arts, only the Bodkin Report can reasonably be considered as directly relevant to efforts to advance the position of the arts. There is but one report which dates from the so-called de Valera years (1932-48). It carries a symbolic title — 'Seasonal Migration to Britain'.

The most noteworthy advances in cultural policy in the period from 1922 to 1950 were the establishment of the Irish Manuscripts Commission (1928) and the Irish Folklore Commission (1935). Both Commissions were, of course, formed as part of the policy of an Irish Ireland. This was also true of the Dublin Institute for Advanced Studies (1940) and of the Irish Placenames Commission (1946).

Isolation during the Emergency encouraged Ireland to change her position. In 1948 the country was finally declared a republic and began to take a more self-assured place in world affairs. It was highly appropriate, therefore, that in 1950 Chester Beatty should arrive in Ireland with an internationally renowned art collection. The Irish Government was beginning to take heed of Bodkin's sharp criticism and it had been decided to establish an independent council to advance the position of the arts. Bodkin hoped to become head of the new council and was prepared to move to Ireland from Great Britain (where he was Professor of Fine Arts at the Barber Institute, Birmingham) if he was offered the post. He wrote to the Taoiseach, John A. Costello:

You must not think that any question of such "prestige" or "honour" as I enjoy there weighs much with me. Just to give you an instance of how little, I may mention that I was invited last Thursday to meet the King and Queen, who were dining with the President of the Royal Academy. The Secretary told me that the guests for the reception afterwards were hand-picked and royally approved and only numbered two hundred. I begged to be excused, not thinking it worth the time, trouble and cost of travelling to London. I would view very differently the honour of working for the Arts in Ireland under the Taoiseach.[12]

This sentiment, the pleasure of being a big fish in a small pond, may well have been in the mind of Chester Beatty when he decided to move to Ireland. Although Bodkin did not return as he had hoped, Beatty arrived in 1950 with a fanfare which announced that he was a very big fish indeed.

Chapter 2

Alfred Chester Beatty: A Brief Biography

I do not think it would be interesting to go into long details — when the baby had its first tooth.

Alfred Chester Beatty

Alfred Chester Beatty's long and interesting career as mining engineer, art collector and philanthropist, can be divided into three distinct phases — the years based in North America (1875-1913), in Great Britain (1913-50), and in the Republic of Ireland (1950-68).

Born in New York on 7 February 1875, the youngest of three sons of John Cuming Beatty and Hetty Bull, he was named after a distant relative, the Reverend Alfred Chester. He disliked the name Alfred and was always known as Chester, giving his signature as 'A. Chester Beatty'.

His Irish ancestry was stronger than he thought. During the 1950s he asked the Irish Genealogical Office to investigate the matter, but the information provided was too slight for the search to be successful. Unknown to Beatty, he had among his family papers some letters which would have made the search easier.[1]

Beatty's mother was of old English colonial stock. Her family had been in America since 1635 when Captain Thomas Bull arrived in Boston on board the 'Hopewell'. Bull became celebrated for his exploits during the Indian Wars and later ancestors were prominent in the struggle for American Independence.[2]

On the paternal side, Beatty's ancestors were Irish. His great-grandparents, David and Anne Beatty, lived in Armagh City and were buried in the Church of Ireland Cathedral there with three of their children.[3] A fourth child, Robert, emigrated to the Danish island of St Thomas in the West Indies but later moved to the United States, settling in New York in 1835.

Robert's wife, Catherine Louisa Armstrong, was a native of Mountrath, County Leix (Laois), the third eldest of eighteen children.[4] She herself bore ten children, seven girls and three boys, one of whom, John Cuming, was Chester Beatty's father. In 1853 Catherine returned to Ireland with two of her children and on 4 June paid a visit to the Beatty family tomb at Armagh Cathedral.[5]

It is more than likely that the Beattys originally came from Scotland. An unverified story relates that a kinsman of the Scottish poet, James Beattie, crossed to Ireland and settled in the town of Hillsborough, County Down. He later adopted to change the spelling of his name to Beatty.

In his brief memoirs, Chester Beatty describes how the Reverend Alfred Chester 'had a mania for collecting minerals, curios, tiny chips of rock from the pyramids, bits of wood supposed to come from Captain Cook's ship, and samples of lead and copper ore . . . and probably this fired my enthusiasm and of course I was the usual collector of postage stamps'.[6] While a pupil at Westminster School, Dobb's Ferry, near the Hudson River, he enjoyed searching for mineral samples on the building sites where tunnels were being driven to carry water to the Cruton Aqueduct in New York City. A friend of Beatty's parents, John C.F. Randolph, a mining engineer, encouraged the young boy to pursue his interest. Mr Randolph was a graduate of Columbia University and Beatty sat the entrance examination there in 1893. He did not enter Columbia University directly, however, first spending a year at Princeton University, as he had decided to accompany his friend and next-door-neighbour, Edward K. Mills, who was going to study civil engineering.

Beatty always remembered this year with affection but as Princeton had no course in mine engineering at the time, he left to enrol as planned at Columbia University School of Mines. His academic excellence soon became clear and in

1898 he received his degree of Engineer of Mines (E.M.) with an average 91% in his final examinations.[7]

Beatty's mining career is a romantic one typical of his profession. Though his family was quite well-to-do (his father was a banker and stockbroker), he refused an allowance from his parents and headed west to Denver, Colorado, with $200 in his pocket and a one-way train ticket. He tried to reassure his mother, who had heard many tales of the Wild West, by showing her a letter of introduction from Mr Randolph which he thought would guarantee him a job. When he arrived at Denver he was disappointed to find that no job awaited him. The only work available was that of 'mucker' or labourer in a mine. He quickly accepted this position from Thomas Arthur Rickard[8] and began his career shovelling rock at the Kekionga Goldmine in Boulder County, Colorado. He received twenty-five cents an hour for a ten-hour day. During the next few years he gained valuable practical experience as he worked his way from 'mucker' to foreman, supervisor to mine manager, mine-owner to millionaire.

When he arrived in Colorado, Beatty soon learned that its mining camps were very influenced by the presence of Irishmen. It is indeed reasonable to ask to what extent Beatty can be considered an Irish-American? He certainly felt at home when he finally settled in Ireland in 1950. His ancestry was clearly part-Irish and he tended to associate with others of similar origin. An analysis of all those whose name and nationality is noted in Beatty's memoirs about his years in America reveals that 53 per cent were Irish-born or of Irish descent. Of 23 mine owners mentioned by Beatty, nine were Irish (39%) and of 39 miners, union officials, sheriffs and judges, 24 were Irish (61%). Recent scholarship has shown that in 1894 one-third of the miners at Cripple Creek, Colorado (where Beatty was working from 1900-03) were Irishmen.[9] Among professional mining engineers like Beatty, the number of Irishmen was fewer than among the labouring miners. Beatty's first boss, T.A. Rickard, wrote a book in 1922 consisting of a series of interviews with 24 mining engineers.[10] Two of those interviewed were Irish-born and four others were of Irish descent (i.e. 25%). Given these statistics, Beatty's career can be seen as an example of the trend of upward mobility in the Irish-American community. He was more privileged than most, having had the benefit of a university education, but he had to start on the bottom rung and work his way up.[11]

Although mining life was rough and dangerous, Beatty found that hard work, courage, discipline and a little luck could yield handsome dividends. Property was won by staking one's claim and profit was seen as a just reward for enterprise.

Beatty often travelled on horseback or by Wells Fargo stagecoach and always carried six-guns at his side and a Colt revolver tucked into his boot (Plate 1). The mining engineer was constantly watching out for mines which had been 'salted' in an effort to dupe the examiner. A good mine was worth a fortune and a mistake by a mining engineer was unacceptable to the exploration companies. Beatty's reputation grew quickly and he came to the attention of John Hays Hammond,[12] the foremost mining engineer of the time.

In 1903 Hammond became chief engineer with the Guggenheim Exploration Company and Beatty was appointed his assistant chief engineer. This important position secured Beatty a salary of $27,000 a year with lucrative investment possibilities, and gave him the opportunity to travel widely throughout the United States of America, Mexico and Canada. In 1906 he personally negotiated a deal with King Leopold II of the Belgians on behalf of the Guggenheim Exploration Company, a contract securing the mineral rights of a huge area of the Congo Free State.

When Beatty's contract with the Guggenheims came up for renewal in 1908, he was offered Hammond's job and asked to name his salary. He refused the offer and, influenced by a legal dispute with the Guggenheims, he chose to open an independent office in New York at 71 Broadway under the title of 'A. Chester Beatty, Consulting Mining Engineer'.[13]

He began to travel extensively and his office business expanded with the help of a group of loyal assistants and associates, some of whom were to remain with him for fifty years. One of these associates was Harold A. Titcomb, who had been Beatty's best friend and classmate at Columbia University School of Mines. They went on many mine examinations

1. Chester Beatty — mining engineer — Colorado, c. 1900.

together and Beatty later liked to describe their adventures in Mexico as they tried to cope with snakes, bandits and sweltering heat. In 1907 Titcomb opened his own office in London and, taking his lead, Beatty began to spend part of the year there too. It was becoming apparent to many mining engineers that London was an ideal centre for mining companies, as it was the focus of the vast British Commonwealth. Beatty was a shrewd businessman, keen to capitalise on any scheme with

2. *Grace Madeleine Rickard (Beatty's first wife).*

potential for profit. It is not unfair to say that at this point in his career he was ruthless. The *Mining Magazine* described him as 'one of the most forceful of the engineer-financier type of men now engaged in mining speculation'.[14] While in London Beatty became acquainted with another mining speculator, Herbert Hoover[15] (later to be 31st President of the United States of America, 1929-33), and together they developed mines in Burma and Russia.

In 1911 Beatty's young wife, Grace Madeleine Rickard (whom he had married in 1900), died of typhoid fever, leaving him with two young children — a daughter Ninette, aged 10, and a son Alfred Chester Junior, aged four.[16] (Plates 2 and 3).

His own health was impaired after years in the underground mines. Suffering from silicosis, he was shocked to have an application for life insurance refused because he was considered unlikely to live more than a few years.

Already a millionaire, Beatty was advised to leave the busy world of mining in the United States and in May 1912 he bought the magnificent Baroda House at 24 Kensington Palace Gardens, London, the former residence of the Gaekwar of the State of Baroda in India.[17] He remarried the following year to Edith Dunn of New York and they settled in London.[18] (Plates 4 and 5). In 1914 a visit to Egypt introduced them to the world of the East and they bought some decorated copies of the Koran in the bazaars. (Plate 6). The dry climate so attracted Beatty that he bought a house near Cairo and spent many winters there over the next twenty-five years.[19]

Having recuperated from illness, Beatty's interest in the potential of the mining industry encouraged him to launch his own mining company called Selection Trust (it was to be 'selective' in its investments). (Plate 7).

The company was launched in December 1914 with a total capital of £20,000, though the First World War (1914-18) delayed the expansion of the enterprise.[20]

Beatty became ill again in 1917, suffering a near fatal attack of pneumonia and Spanish influenza. His doctors advised him to go to a warm climate to recover and so, despite the Great War, Beatty embarked on a world health cruise. Accompanied by his wife and daughter, he spent four months in Japan and

3. Ninette Beatty (daughter).

4. Baroda House, 24 Kensington Palace Gardens, London.

travelled to China. He had long been fascinated by certain Oriental art objects and by 1914 he owned a superb collection of Chinese snuff bottles.[21] His interest in art was inspired by his pleasure in the natural beauty of mineral samples and this led to an admiration for snuff bottles made from semi-precious stones. One can determine a gradual sophistication in Beatty's artistic taste as his interest in Chinese snuff bottles, Japanese decorative arts, Oriental rugs and Arabic manuscripts encouraged him to visit the East. He generously regarded the East as encompassing all places from Moorish Spain to the North of Africa, all the way to Japan and Indonesia.

5. Edith Dunn (Beatty's second wife).

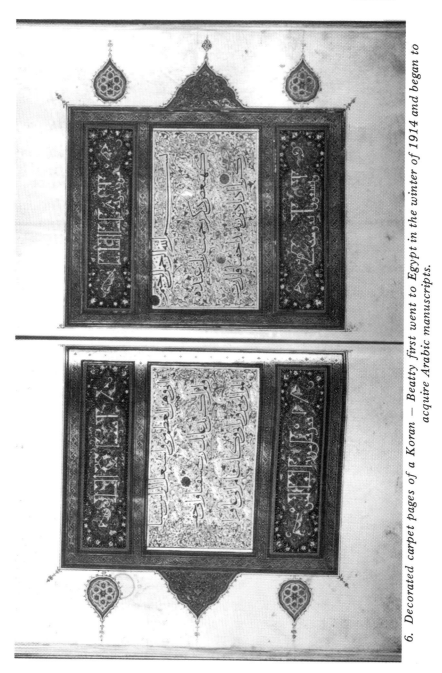

6. *Decorated carpet pages of a Koran — Beatty first went to Egypt in the winter of 1914 and began to acquire Arabic manuscripts.*

7. The offices of Selection Trust, Mason's Avenue, London.

Travels in Egypt and the Far East fuelled Beatty's interest and he returned from every trip with fine examples of Oriental craftsmanship and artistry. He began to organise his art collecting in a similar manner to the organisation of his mining activities; the subject was vetted by experts, examined for forgery, a fair price given, only the highest quality accepted,

31

and the final decision rested with Beatty himself. He was encouraged by his wife Edith, a strong-minded and remarkable lady whose many interests included Western illuminated manuscripts, antique furniture, post mid-nineteenth century European painting (especially French Impressionists), and thorough-bred racehorses! (Plate 8).

As Beatty's art collections expanded at a phenomenal rate in the 1920s, Selection Trust also surged forward to become a group of companies with mining interests in many countries including Russia, Serbia, Gold Coast and Sierra Leone. The greatest revenue was generated in Africa and specifically in Northern Rhodesia (now Zambia), where Rhodesian Selection Trust controlled much of the rich copper belt. (Plate 9).

Beatty contributed to mining technology by helping to pioneer new methods of extracting copper from low-grade ore. His business flair was based on courage, expertise and an ability to delegate responsibility. He dared to explore and exploit the copper reserves of Africa where others had lost fortunes in previous ventures and the geography and climate were generally considered impossible for successful mining. Using new mining techniques and concentrating on housing and health care for his staff, Beatty was amply rewarded for his enterprise, becoming one of the wealthiest men in Great Britain. (Plate 10). His profession acknowledged his achievement with many honours, including the Gold Medal of the Institute of Mining and Metallurgy (1935). In 1930 he received the Grand Cordon of the Order of St Sava for his work in developing Yugoslavia's mining resources. Two years later he was awarded the Order of King Leopold II for his services in developing the Belgian Congo.

Although modest about his mining success, Beatty was justifiably proud of his art collections. He was adamant that he was not a scholar, but fifty years of careful study and the vetting of high quality art material allowed him to become very knowledgeable. Beatty had complete confidence in his own eye for quality and this was to be the hallmark of the Chester Beatty Library. Its founder considered quality to mean, first and foremost, good condition. Other factors were then considered: rarity, value, age, aesthetic or artistic merit.

8. The drawing room, Baroda House, London — oriental carpet, French eighteenth century furnitue and Impressionist/Post Impressionist paintings including Van Gogh's 'Sunflowers' (inset) which fetched £25 million at a Christie's auction on 30 March 1987.

Beatty would often reject material on the grounds that it was 'unhealthy' or 'grubby'.[22] He had his own system of note-taking while visiting a museum or a dealer's shop. For example, if he did not wish to buy an item or would not wish to own it, he would write 'D.C.F.I.' meaning 'Don't Care For It' or 'N.F.F.C.' meaning 'Not Fit For Collection'. Everything that he bought was classed as 'A', 'B' or 'C' according to quality.

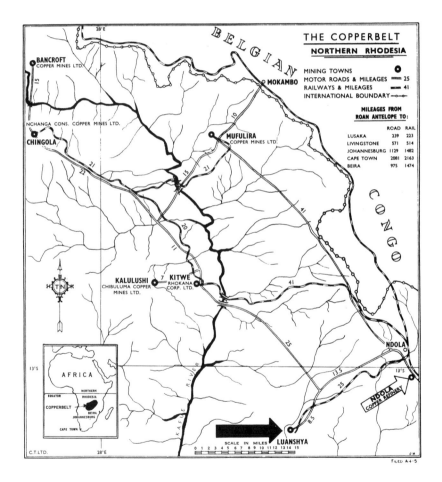

9. *Map showing the major mines operated by Rhodesian Selection Trust in Northern Rhodesia (now Zambia). The mines were nationalised in 1970.*

10. Chester Beatty — a captain of British industry, c. 1935.

A most discriminating buyer, he rarely purchased at random or in bulk. He did not speak or read any of the many Oriental languages represented in his collections; this encouraged the purchase of illustrated material, fine bindings and an admiration for beautiful calligraphy. For this reason the Chester Beatty collections cannot adequately be described as a library, more often resembling a museum or an art gallery.

In 1933 Beatty became a naturalised British citizen. Two years earlier he had attracted public attention in Great Britain when he gave material on loan to the International Exhibition of Persian Art held at Burlington House in London, and especially in November when it was announced in *The Times* that he had acquired some biblical papyri which, in the words of Sir Frederic Kenyon, retired Director of the British Museum, constituted 'the most remarkable addition to the textual material of the Greek Bible which has been made for many a long day'.[23] The discovery was generally agreed to include some of the earliest known papyrus copies of the New Testament. Beatty had them restored, mounted, researched by eminent scholars, and reproduced in fine catalogues. (Plate 11).

Recognised as a captain of industry, Beatty soon established himself as a major patron of the arts. He supported many British libraries, museums and universities, presented gifts to the British Museum[24] and to the Victoria and Albert Museum[25] and was well acquainted with museum staff, scholars and the art world generally. The range and quality of the Chester Beatty collections became apparent to the British art public through the various exhibitions which he supported — Chinese Art (1935), French Book Illustration (1945), the Arts of India (1947), Biblical Manuscripts (1948), and many other smaller exhibitions.

Among Beatty's charitable activities in Great Britain was his support for the cause of cancer research. In 1939 he acquired a building on the Fulham Road in London and after defraying the cost of complete modernisation, presented it to the Royal Cancer Hospital, of which he was then President (founded in 1851, it is now called the Royal Marsden Hospital).

In 1929 Beatty had enlisted the help of the celebrated anti-malaria specialist, Sir Malcolm Watson (of the Ross Institute of Tropical Hygiene, London), to devise a plan for the Northern

11. Gospel of St John, x, 7-25 and xi, 42-57 — 3rd
century papyrus codex
(courtesy of the Trustees of the CBL).

Rhodesian copper belt.[26] The campaign was very successful and death rates of both European and African employees dropped dramatically within a few years. Many British companies in Africa followed Beatty's example by introducing health care schemes. Similarly in London, Selection Trust was one of the first companies to introduce comprehensive health, holiday and pension schemes for its staff.

Beatty's greatest contribution to Great Britain came during the Second World War (1939-45). He committed himself to the Allied war effort and was appointed to a number of Government committees established by the Ministry of Supply, becoming a member of the Non-Ferrous Metals Sub-Committee and of the Diamond Dies Advisory Sub-Committee. When the British Government formed the United Kingdom Commercial Corporation (U.K.C.C.) in April 1940 to further the war-time trade effort and ensure the supply of necessary raw materials, Beatty was appointed a Director and Vice-Chairman, with particular responsibility for the supply of minerals and the transport of bulk materials.[27] (Plate 12). He was appointed Chairman of U.K.C.C. (Portugal), Chairman of Selection Manufacturing Company Ltd. (engaged in the manufacture of certain war weapons), and Vice-Chairman of the London Committee of the Yugoslav Red Cross Society.

For the duration of the war, Beatty lived in a suite at the Grosvenor Hotel in Park Lane because Baroda House was being used as a hospital (during the First World War Baroda House had become American Red Cross Hospital Number Twenty-Four). While serving on the various Government committees, he continued to direct the affairs of his mining companies. He wrote to a friend:

> I am very glad to say that I am keeping very fit, in spite of the fact that I have to work harder than I have done for many years. I am by no means depressed by the news. We must expect setbacks from time to time and I am confident that if anyone can steer us to victory, Churchill is the one to do it.[28]

It should be remembered that, like Churchill, Beatty had reached the age of sixty-five by the outbreak of the Second World War.

In 1943 Beatty's villa near Cairo, Bait el Azrak, was used as Churchill's residence during important discussions prior to the Teheran conference between Churchill, Roosevelt, Smuts and Chiang Kai-Shek.[29] Beatty also made the staff and facilities of his mining companies available for service at the discretion of the British Government.

The many war-time activities in which Beatty was personally involved included ensuring the supply of wolfram (used to harden the steel of tanks and shells), providing diamond dies (necessary for making copper wire), organising the supply route to Russia via Persia, and planning the aborted 'Operation Danube' using dynamite from his Yugoslav mines to dam the great river.[30]

12. Some of the Directors of the United Kingdom Commercial Corporation (U.K.C.C.), 1940.

Sir Frank Nixon *L.C. Paton* *C.P. Lister* *E.J. Shearer*

J.H. Hambro Capt. J.A. Leighton A. Chester Beatty G.A. McEwen

In April 1945 Beatty wrote: 'Things are quiet in London now the V2s have stopped, and the war going marvellously. I do not think it will be very long before it is over'.[31] The following month the war in Europe ended with the surrender of the German armies. Beatty, tired and weary after six strenuous years in London, hoped to escape quickly to his villa in Egypt for the sake of his health. He did not manage to leave until 1946 and, in the meantime, he was to be most disturbed by post-war political changes in Great Britain.

Chapter 3

The Move from Great Britain to the Republic of Ireland

That is no country for old men.

W.B. Yeats

The Background in Great Britain 1945-50

The immediate post-war period in Europe was characterised by a general political swing to the left. In Great Britain the election results announced on 25 July 1945 were a welcome surprise to the Labour Party, a profound shock to the Conservatives. In a landslide victory the Labour Party won a parliamentary majority for the first time in British history.[1]

The new Government inherited the difficult task of managing the post-war balance of payments situation. Hugh Dalton, M.P., Chancellor of the Exchequer (until 1947) told the House of Commons that Britain had started the war with debts of £496 million and ended it with debts of £3,500 million.[2] But whereas in 1939 the country had vast reserves in gold, dollars and overseas investments, it had by 1945 been almost entirely stripped of these.

Given this situation, the late 1940s in Great Britain were to be marked by austerity programmes under the guidance of Sir Stafford Cripps (President of the Board of Trade 1945-7 and Chancellor of the Exchequer 1947-50), but also by radically innovative schemes led by Aneurin 'Nye' Bevan (Minister of Health 1945-51). A year after taking office the

41

Prime Minister, Clement Attlee, was able to tell the Labour Party Conference in Bournemouth (June 1946) that 75 Bills had already been introduced and 55 had received the Royal Assent. 'In previous Parliaments', he said, 'any one of these would have been thought a full meal for a year'.[3] Not surprisingly, supporters of the Conservative Party thought that the world had been turned upside down.

It can be safely assumed that Chester Beatty supported the Conservative Party.[4] He was a firm believer in free enterprise, convinced of the civilising influence of the 'white man' in the colonies, and a friend of many of the wealthiest people in Great Britain. His hero was Winston Churchill, whom he called 'a real artist, a versatile man, the greatest of our time, with the courage of a lion'.[5] (Plate 13). When the imposing war-time leader was rejected by the British electorate in 1945, Beatty felt, like many other Tory supporters, that an alien philosophy was beginning to take hold in the country — the idea that 'Jack was as good as his master'.

The Labour Party manifesto *Let Us Face The Future* had insisted that 'Labour will plan from the ground up'. Attlee called the process 'levelling up', which meant helping as many proletarians as possible to achieve his own middle-class standards. He was essentially conservative-minded and was regarded with disdain by many in his party when he accepted an Earldom for services rendered. Unlike Attlee (the son of a well-to-do London solicitor), Aneurin 'Nye' Bevan typified the new aggressive Labour spirit. A former Welsh miner who had left school at the age of 13, Bevan was a superb orator with a capacity for devastating wit, and through his outspoken style he came to symbolise, for the Tories, all that was wrong with the new Government. Beatty enjoyed quoting the joke that the 'Welfare State' was more akin to the 'Farewell State'.

On 4 July 1948, Bevan delivered a fiery speech at Belle Vue, Manchester.[6] He contrasted the Labour Party's social programme with the sad memories of his own youth on the Means Test and told his audience:

No amount of cajolery can eradicate from my heart a deep burning hatred for the Tory Party that inflicted those experiences on me. So far as I am concerned they are lower than vermin. They condemned millions of first-class people to semi-starvation.

13. Winston Churchill.

Bevan saw nothing unusual in this rhetoric, but the next day the newspapers reported the speech under headlines such as 'Mr Bevan's Bitter Attack on Conservatives' (*Manchester Guardian*); 'Bevan: I Hate the Tories' (*Daily Express*); and 'Mr Bevan's Burning Hatred. Attack on Tory "vermin" ' (*The Times*). The headline in *The Times* had caught the provocative word 'vermin' and soon every Tory in Britain was discussing the appalling Mr Bevan. The following Friday night someone daubed across the outside of Bevan's house at 23 Clivedon Place, the inscription 'Vermin Villa — Home of a Loud-Mouthed Rat'. The *Sunday Dispatch* captured the flavour of the week with the banner headline: 'The Man Who Hates 8,093,858 People', that being the number of people who voted Conservative at the 1945 election.

Churchill joined the foray by characterising Bevan as 'The Minister of Disease'. Bevan reacted brilliantly:

> When I speak of Tories I mean the small bodies of people who, whenever they have the chance, have manipulated the political influence of the country for the benefit of the privileged few . . . I am not prepared to forget and forgive the wrongs done to my people. We need twenty years of power to transfer the citadels of capitalism from the hands of a few people to the control of the nation. Only after twenty years can we afford to be polite. Then maybe I won't have enough energy to be rude, but while we have the energy let us be rude to the right people.

The prospect of 20 years of changes on the scale of those instituted by the Labour Party from 1945 to 1948 must have horrified Tory supporters like Chester Beatty. He rarely referred to politics when writing letters because, as a successful businessman, he believed that politicians do not hold the real power in a country. Wealth controls power — he who pays the piper calls the tune. But the efforts of men like Bevan to change the structure of British society worried Beatty very deeply. The 'vermin speech' was remembered long after the initial controversy had died down. It was a crude jibe which hurt the Tory consciousness.

In September 1950 Beatty went to London for a retirement dinner organised in his honour by the Directors of Selection Trust. He good-humouredly introduced his speech with the words, 'Vermin and Old Friends from Overseas'.[7] (Plate 14). He explained:

> The first name I use as from what I can see you come under the classification according to the Minister of Health, and he should know as he is trying to stamp out vermin. Also, I do not see any Socialists or Communists here tonight, so I am afraid we all come under this classification. But in thinking of the abuse showered upon us I cannot help thinking of that little poem:

14. *Beatty's retirement dinner, 27 September 1950. His son, A. Chester Beatty Junior, is seated to his immediate left.*

The Bee, a busy little soul,
Has just no time for Birth Control,
So hence in Whitehall now one sees
So many, many Sons of B's.

Beatty described the start of his career at the Kekionga
Goldmine in Colorado:

We struck ore and the mine got on a paying basis, and
then I had more work than I could handle. I opened an
office in Denver and started raising my fees as a Consulting Engineer and I have been raising them ever since.
Lately I started reducing them, and if Stafford Cripps
continues I will soon get back to my old rate.

Beatty ended his speech by wishing his audience God's
blessing in Irish: 'Bail O Dhia oraibh go léir'. He saw some of
his audience wonder at the use of this 'strange language', so
he translated the greeting for them. Many of the distinguished
guests must have wondered at a lot more than the use of Irish.
They could not understand why Beatty should wish to leave
London at all. Ireland certainly seemed to them to be an odd
site for a splendid collection of Oriental art. The *Sunday
Express* noted that 'Friends and associates in London cannot
explain the move of this American-born magnate'.[8]

Two reasons are generally advanced to explain Beatty's
decision to leave Great Britain. Firstly, as told by Sheila
Wingfield (Lady Powerscourt), it is said that he left the
country because of difficulty in obtaining foreign currency
to go abroad for health reasons after the Second World War.[9]
J.V.S. Wilkinson (Beatty's Librarian from 1946 to 1957) is
given as the source for this explanation. Arthur Wilson has
accepted Wilkinson's story and has added: 'It was this, more
than anything else, that set him [Beatty] thinking about
emigrating for the second time'.[10] The implications of this
statement have, however, been ignored.

The Republic of Ireland was a member of the Sterling
Area and its residents were subject to exchange control like
their counterparts in Great Britain.[11] On 22 January 1952,
the Irish Government further restricted exchange control by
introducing measures including a £50 basic exchange allowance

for holiday travel outside the Sterling Area.[12] This was precisely the measure which Wilkinson gave as the reason for Beatty's departure from Great Britain.

It is obvious that there was little advantage in Beatty moving to Ireland for currency reasons unless he knew that the Irish Government intended to offer him special privileges. He knew how to find his way around the British regulations but he abhored the bureaucratic labyrinth which had to be negotiated in order to achieve his wishes. What he hoped for, more than anything else, was a change of attitude. He disliked the lack of respect shown to people of his wealth, experience and influence, under the Labour Government. He expected that special provision would be made for people like him. In May 1949 Beatty went to Dublin to discuss this problem with Frederick H. Boland, Secretary of the Irish Department of External Affairs. He found, much to his delight, that the attitude of the Irish authorities was a highly sympathetic one.

The second reason which is generally given to explain Beatty's move to Dublin is that he had a row with the Director of the British Museum.[13] It is told that the Director, Sir John Forsdyke, refused to agree to retain Beatty's Library as a separate unit if he were to present it to the British Museum. This explanation contains an element of truth but it is, nevertheless, an unsatisfactory reason why Beatty should leave Great Britain. It certainly does not explain Beatty's removal to the Republic of Ireland.

The Decision to Leave Great Britain
Red-Tape and Rules

In 1949 when Beatty decided to leave London and move to Dublin he was already 74 years of age. He joked that it was time for the old miner to go off shift. Selection Trust had come through a difficult period, but with the devaluation of sterling in September 1949 the price of copper rose dramatically and the prosperity of the African copper belt was assured.[14] Beatty had always been a master of delegation and had gradually given over the day-to-day running of his group of companies to a number of capable businessmen, including

47

his son Alfred Chester Junior ('Chet'). He wished to devote his retirement years to consolidating his art collections and to guaranteeing their future after his death. He could, of course, have arranged to bequeath his Library to a British institution or he could have established an independent foundation in Great Britain. The main reason he chose not to do so was his growing dislike, throughout the 1940s, of the policies of the Labour Party Government.

Clement Attlee had said that it was Labour's function in Britain to be the accelerator, Conservatism's to act as the brake.[15] But during the 1940s and 1950s British society seemed to have taken off with a momentum of its own — an automatic fuel-feed. It was a very different society to that which Beatty had known and not one for which he had much sympathy.

Social change coincided with the innovative policies which were being introduced by Attlee's Government. Many people considered that the State was concerning itself with far more than it either could or should. Beatty complained that life was becoming 'too regulated'.[16] He explained that his reasons for leaving Britain were 'red-tape, regimentation and controls'.[17] At the Annual General Meeting of Selection Trust in 1949 he was reported as having said that London was no longer the centre of the mining world. The position would deteriorate while high taxation, unjust duties and rigid controls stopped new mining projects from being launched.[18] Sir Ronald Prain, Managing Director of Rhodesian Selection Trust, has described a typical board meeting chaired by Beatty during the late 1940s:

> He exuded good humour and jollity and usually opened the meeting with some amusing remarks. His favourite subject was the evil of bureaucracy and his dislike of the Socialist Government which was then in office. He would speak at great length on the virtues of private enterprise and would hold the board spellbound for a long time before anyone thought of making a start on the agenda.[19]

Bureaucracy and regulations infuriated Beatty. He had never allowed such impediments to interrupt the work of his mining companies and he could not understand why any

48

government should encourage such inefficiency. When a friend sent him a gift of cigars, he had to write back explaining that the reason for the delay in offering his thanks was his 'great trouble with the British Customs Authorities'. He said he was fed up with forms and obstructions and there was too much 'red-tape about export'.[20]

Beatty's difficulty regarding foreign currency for travel abroad did not begin immediately after the Second World War. It has been stated, incorrectly, that Beatty never visited Egypt again due to the severity of exchange control regulations.[21] In fact Beatty visited Bait el Azrak on another two occasions.

The reason why Beatty was unable to visit Egypt in 1945, as he had hoped, was not due to currency shortages but to his wife's ill health.[22] In the spring of 1946 he went to Switzerland and visited Dr Martin Bodmer, a friend and fellow art collector.[23] Bodmer complained that almost three-quarters of his fortune was blocked in the United States: 'That's the wonderful new freedom of our developed civilisation.'[24] Beatty sympathised: 'The American attitude vis-à-vis Switzerland is most unreasonable and appallingly short-sighted and stupid. Here in England I think they take quite an enlightened view.'[25] Beatty offered to use his own sterling if Bodmer heard of anything in the London salesrooms which he liked.[26] Obviously, Beatty was not yet finding the currency regulations too difficult.

During the summer of 1946 Mr and Mrs Beatty went to Vichy and spent a week in Paris visiting the dealers' shops. They had to return quickly to London when his wife became very ill.[27] Edith Beatty remained at Baroda House until her death in 1952. Her husband continued to support her financially but strained marital relations must be considered as a factor in Beatty's decision to leave London.[28]

Currency regulations changed dramatically in 1947 when the Exchange Control Act was introduced to restrict the purpose for which foreign currency or gold could be sold or retained. At first there was a £75 foreign exchange allowance for persons going abroad, but this was soon reduced to £50 worth of foreign currency per annum.

The debates in the House of Commons on the Exchange

Control Bill were marked by strongly condemnatory speeches by Conservative Party M.P.s, one of whom argued: 'There is no doubt that this Bill will make Great Britain a prison'.[29] Viscount Hinchingbrooke, M.P., reflected Beatty's opinion when he claimed that the Labour Party was 'too wedded to the beliefs of the bureaucratic planners'.[30] Mr Drayson, M.P., suggested provocatively that the Bill was 'a new instrument in the Chancellor's torture chamber with which he can harass the exporter and the businessman ... nothing more than Fascist finance to bolster up Socialist insolvency'.[31]

The scale of the British war debts dictated high taxation policies which were not designed to please wealthy business-men like Beatty. The highest rate of surtax ever charged in Great Britain was 10s. 6d. in the pound, which was enforced in the years from 1946 to 1951 on the excess of total income over £20,000. Given this punitive rate, it is reasonable to ask if Chester Beatty was better off financially by moving to the Republic of Ireland. While little of his correspondence regard-ing his personal finances (taxation, applications for currency, ownership of stocks and shares) survives, it is nevertheless possible to compare the tax rates in force in the two countries. Furthermore, the Double Taxation Relief Agreement[32] meant that if Beatty became an Irish resident he was only liable to tax in that country. He would be subject to the Irish rates of income tax and surtax, and exempt from British tax on all property situated and of gains or profits arising in Great Britain or Northern Ireland.

It is hardly surprising to find that Beatty was substantially better off by choosing to reside in Dublin. In the year 1949/50 the British standard rate of income tax was 9s. 0d. and sur-tax 10s. 6d.; the comparative Irish rates were 6s. 6d. and 8s. 6d. Thus British residents with incomes over £20,000 bore tax at 19s. 6d. in the pound, while in the Republic of Ireland similar residents bore tax at 15s. 0d. in the pound. In brief, Beatty was 25 per cent better off financially by the move to Dublin. His accountants may well have been able to negotiate the complicated system of reliefs and credits to his further advantage.[33]

The truth of the second reason advanced to explain Beatty's move to Ireland arose not so much because of a row with the

Director of the British Museum, but due to the tightening up of regulations regarding the import and export of manuscripts.

Beatty had long been a friend of the British Museum, making donations of money and gifts of art works over a period of 40 years. His own art collections were built on the premise: 'I want to compare our collection with the British Museum collection of the same class of material'.[34] James Wilkinson had worked at the British Museum for 22 years before he became Beatty's Librarian in 1946. When Beatty went to Cairo during the winter of 1946/7, he did not see any need to alter his former habit of sending manuscripts to Wilkinson care of the British Museum. He wrote: 'I thought that was better than the Baroda address'.[35] There were fewer customs difficulties if manuscripts were sent to the Museum and Beatty was exporting Arabic manuscripts against the wishes of the Egyptian Government.

Beatty was naturally secretive about his actions and warned Wilkinson: 'By the way, *don't forget* we *never buy any Korans* in Egypt because it will be impossible to get permission from the Government to export them'.[36] He then proceeded to send Wilkinson 15 rare texts, some Korans and some big sectional Korans.

It must not be concluded that Beatty exported manuscripts illegally on a regular basis. He generally tried to keep within the letter of the law but he considered that, as in other areas, the law was becoming too restrictive. He wrote to Wilkinson: 'Sorry to hear that you are having such a hard time in England. The Labour Party are certainly making a success of things???? What a mess!!!'.[37]

In April 1947 Beatty was most annoyed when the British Museum created a fuss about a number of Armenian manuscripts which he had sent to Wilkinson care of the Museum. Perhaps innocently enough, it was thought that the manuscripts were intended for the Museum's collections. Beatty was furious when the Foreign Office was alerted and it became known that the manuscripts were destined for his own Library at Baroda House. In this instance Beatty had not broken any rules or regulations. Egyptian law only prohibited the export of papyri and Arabic manuscripts. Beatty was unimpressed by the efforts of the Director of the British Museum, Sir

John Forsdyke, to resolve the matter. He wrote bitterly:

> When I get back I will have a straight talk with the
> Director. They can't have it both ways. Court presents
> from me help them in the auctions and then when you
> send something care of them they seem to object. In
> future I will ask no favours and give none . . . The BM
> is more under obligation to me than I am to them and
> we do not need or want their help in the future.[38]

Beatty found that the obstacles to successful art collecting
had increased. The Egyptian Government was beginning to
enforce regulations which it had in former years been easy to
circumvent.

In the winter of 1949/50, Beatty returned to Egypt to take
a last look at the market for manuscripts. It was as he had
suspected in 1946/7: 'The collecting of rare Arabic manuscripts here is practically finished . . . but personally I do not
regret it, as I think now at my age to call a halt and to concentrate on finishing the catalogues'.[39]

The belief that his collecting days were over strongly
influenced Beatty's decision to provide for the future of his
library. He knew that the type of collection which he had
brought together could not easily be repeated, as export
regulations were tightened and as art collectors in the United
States pushed prices out of reach.[40] It was no longer as
much fun to collect manuscripts. Beatty felt suffocated by
red-tape and rules. The British Museum affair had been the
last straw. He told Wilkinson that it had not been his fault
and advised: 'Don't worry about the B.M. We have got so
many Bureaucrats that they have to be busy doing something
so that is why they are so keen to know what everyone is
doing'.[41]

Baroda House caused a further problem for Beatty. Besides
the fact that his estranged wife was living there, the house
had been built on Crown land almost opposite Kensington
Palace. It was a splendid house but had become too small
to hold Beatty's art collections. On the two occasions when
planning permission had been sought to extend the building,
Beatty had experienced difficulties. Wilkinson became irri-
tated when a proposal for an extension was again rejected

in the spring of 1949. He wrote to John Wooderson (Beatty's private business secretary in London), complaining of valuable books lying about on tables or on congested shelves:

> The present state of things is really unworthy of such a wonderful library . . . I have made so many proposals in the last two and a half years which have all come to nothing and it would be a great satisfaction to get something accomplished.[42]

Beatty knew that alternative accommodation was necessary. He was concerned after his experience in London during the Second World War that he should never have to repeat the evacuation of his art treasures. But where would he find a suitable 'quiet spot'[43] free of bureaucracy?

Why Dublin?

No comment is more revealing of Beatty's attitude to Ireland than his assertion that 'Ireland is the best country in the world in which to retire. The country has atmosphere. The people have so much charm — life goes on as it did elsewhere until 1939'.[44] Whatever this comment may indicate about the Irish capacity for work, it demonstrates Beatty's opinion that the more conservative Irish society was infinitely preferable to the so-called 'New Britain'.

Although Beatty was aware that he had Irish ancestry, there is no evidence that he gave it any consideration until the late 1940s. After he moved to Ireland he sometimes recalled stories which he had been told as a young boy by his grandmother Catherine Armstrong. He also recounted tales of his days in the mining communities of Colorado and the Irishmen who figured so prominently there.

These factors may have influenced Beatty to some extent but it was his own visits to Ireland which confirmed his liking for the country. He first visited Dublin in late August 1937, staying at the Shelbourne Hotel, and he and his wife spent some time in the antique shops along the quays.[45] Beatty said that he found Dublin to be an agreeable old-world city.[46]

After the Second World War some of Beatty's friends told him about enjoyable holidays in Ireland. Colonel David Bruce wrote of an exciting 'woodcock and snipe rough shoot' and added that the new air route to Ireland had made the journey very pleasant.[47] As Aer Lingus embarked on an expansion programme after the war, the increased accessibility made Ireland more attractive to wealthy Britons who wanted a quiet weekend retreat but did not wish to spend hours travelling there.

In 1948 Alfred Chester Beatty Junior bought a large eighteenth-century house and estate called Mount Armstrong at Donadea, County Kildare.[48] His father came to visit on a number of occasions and enjoyed meeting members of his son's social circle. He himself had no personal friends in Ireland but nevertheless he decided that he would like to live there. His decision required courage and enthusiasm, not that he lacked either, and once he had made the choice he pursued his objective with vigour.

In 1949 Beatty made two visits to Dublin in order to sound out the likely official reaction in Ireland if he decided to move there. During the first visit Beatty arranged to meet the Secretary of the Department of External Affairs, Frederick Boland. They met for lunch on 16 June and Beatty found Boland to be 'a man of civilised taste' and 'very co-operative'.[49]

Boland has been described as 'a sagacious and experienced diplomatist'[50] and a 'formidable secretary'.[51] He was to become Beatty's main contact in the first year following the decision to move to Ireland. The memorandum which Boland wrote on 29 June 1950, regarding his interview with Beatty, is of great interest as an explanation of Beatty's decision and as an indication of the special treatment which he was to receive from the Irish Government.[52]

Beatty was introduced to Boland in a letter from Lord Rugby (Sir John Maffey, British Representative in Ireland, 1939-49), which stated that Beatty was 'now the world "Copper King" and is probably worth £10 million'. Boland understood that Beatty had 'made a hobby of collecting pictures and Oriental MSS' which he intended to transfer from London to Dublin if he could obtain the necessary export licences from the British Government. Beatty wished to present a collection of pictures to the Irish nation and to build a private museum for his Oriental manuscripts 'which he would endow so as to provide for its continuance after his death'. (Plate 15). With these promises it could be said that Beatty bought his way into Ireland. Boland's memorandum continued:

Mr Beatty's reasons for choosing Ireland as the object of these benevolent intentions were, firstly, that he claims to be of Irish origin, two of his grandfathers having been born in this country; secondly, dislike of the current policies of the Socialist Government in Britain; and thirdly, the belief that this country has a better chance ... of escaping destruction in the event of war than Britain. He mentioned on one occasion that it was the Aga Khan who first put it into his head to locate his collections in Ireland.[53]

Beatty explained that he had resigned all his directorships in favour of his son and had purchased a residence at 10 Ailesbury Road in Dublin, where he intended to live when he was not in the South of France (Plate 16). He asked Boland to find out if the Irish Government would accept the gift of his collection of French nineteenth-century pictures. Boland concluded by noting that 'Mr Beatty, who is a Protestant, seems to be in touch with Trinity College' about his collection of manuscripts and 'he indicated, semi-jocularly, in the course of conversation with Mr McGreevy, that he would be prepared to consider buying pictures (e.g. Velasquez) to fill serious existing gaps in the National Gallery'.[54]

The Irish Government and senior civil servants must have wondered at the arrival of Chester Beatty as much as, if not more than, Beatty's friends in Great Britain had been puzzled by his decision to leave that country. But Beatty promised such important benefactions that Irish officialdom put its wonder aside and adopted a policy of nurturing the intentions which he had declared. Beatty knew his tax position would improve when he moved to Dublin but finance was not his major concern. He would be a willing philanthropist if he received the respect and consideration which had not been accorded him in 'Socialist Britain'.

At Boland's instigation, the official reaction to Beatty's arrival in Ireland was most hospitable indeed. He began by

15. Illustrated page from the Turkish manuscript History of the Sultan Suleiman the Magnificent (1579). (Courtesy Trustees of the CBL).

16. Beatty's Dublin residence at 10 Ailesbury Road.

alerting other government departments of Beatty's intentions. In a confidential letter to Maurice Moynihan, Secretary of the Department of the Taoiseach, he wrote with some humour and undisguised intent:

> Mr Beatty is a person of considerable wealth and obviously benevolent intentions, based to some extent perhaps on the feeling that it is better to have the pleasure of spending money when one is alive rather than leave it to be handed over by one's executors in the form of estate duty. On general grounds, therefore, he is a person worth encouraging . . . What has to be considered now, I think, is what official steps should be taken in connection with the matter.[55]

Boland suggested that he should chair an informal conference to be attended by Mr McGreevy of the National Gallery and the Secretaries of the Departments of the Taoiseach, Finance and Education.

Few people can have entered Ireland to such high level reaction, but during the next 18 years Beatty amply repaid the compliment as he assumed the role of 'Patron of the Arts'. As an enthusiastic and dynamic personality, Beatty came to Ireland with all sorts of interesting ideas for the encouragement of the arts. In Dublin, he felt that he had a personal opportunity to help a city to become a great focus of cultural activity. Boland wrote to Kathleen O'Connell, Private Secretary to Mr de Valera, informing her that Beatty wished to discuss his ideas with the Taoiseach. Beatty believed:

> that Dublin should replace Munich as the repository of Europe's principal archaeological treasures as being the safest and most stable European capital. He would like to help to make Dublin a great cultural centre. He also told me that he has been in correspondence for some time with wealthy Irish-American friends of his in the United States with a view to the establishment of an Irish-American Foundation whose object it would be to develop Dublin in this way.[56]

Leaving Dublin officials to ponder such optimistic ideas, Beatty returned to London. He was delighted with Boland's response and arranged to send him a gift of his *Catalogue of Indian Miniatures*.[57] But when he told his close friends of his intention to move to Dublin they were so astonished that he decided not to announce his decision publicly. He was afraid that the British Government might put a Barring Order on the export of some of his art treasures. Wilkinson warned him: 'It is just possible that somebody will raise a protest about the papyri leaving the country, if it is known that you are settling in Ireland'.[58]

The move to Ireland came as a great personal surprise to Wilkinson. He had never been to the country and feared that he would lose contact with his scholar-friends in London. He could not see any sense in establishing an Oriental library in Dublin, as it would be an isolated if decorative institution. In contrast, London was a renowned centre of Oriental studies — the move just did not make sense.

Wilkinson wrote to his friend Arthur Arberry (Professor of Arabic at Cambridge):

> I especially want to talk to you about a very important step which Mr Beatty is resolved on. Prepare yourself for a shock! He is going to move his library to Ireland and contemplates sending MSS, etc. over by plane. I think you will like to talk to him about this as I foresee endless impediments to work.[59]

Arberry replied: 'It is a shocking shock!' He consoled Wilkinson by adding that the move would mean 'a nice house for you in Dublin, and plenty of food to make up for these dreadful years. That would be the best part of the move and I should be most happy for you. It is all too puzzling to make out at the moment'.[60] Arberry took the liberty of informing Beatty about Wilkinson's concern 'about the high cost of living in Dublin and the financial implications of his move'.[61] Though rationing was less severe with food and luxury goods more accessible to well-off people in Dublin, the cost of living was 36% higher than in London.[62] Beatty reassured his librarian by doubling his salary and they began to prepare for the move in earnest.

In September they visited Dublin for three days to examine the warehouses of Miller & Beatty Ltd. of Grafton Street and found them to be 'wonderfully dry' and 'up-to-date'.[63] During the next few months the Chester Beatty collections were flown to Dublin and deposited with Miller & Beatty. It was a mammoth task — 35 tons of art works packed in 250 boxes. As each consignment arrived in Dublin Wilkinson heaved a sigh of relief, since he did not share Beatty's enthusiasm about the safety of airplanes.

While Beatty left for his winter vacation in Egypt, his worried librarian was left to take care of removal arrangements, export papers and the enquiries of curious journalists. He tried to ignore inquisitive newspaper reporters who were eager to know if the rumours of Beatty's imminent departure were true. On 6 November 1949, the *Sunday Express* printed an article with the bold headline 'Copper King Ships Out

£1,000,000 Treasures'. Wilkinson was disgusted and wrote to Beatty:

> The article is, of course, fantastic and vulgar, but it is rather unfortunate that it should appear now. I thought I had ridden off the little man . . . The only redeeming features are that the papyri are not mentioned, and the Dublin library is not, apparently, known of.[64]

However, 'fantastic and vulgar', the *Sunday Express* article succeeded in alerting the authorities in Great Britain of Beatty's intention to leave the country. It was not long before Beatty received a letter from the Archbishop of Canterbury (Geoffrey Fisher, Archbishop 1945-61), who was one of the three Principal Trustees of the British Museum.[65]

The Archbishop wrote that he had been informed that at one time Beatty had considered giving his 'immensely valuable Biblical Papyri and Manuscripts' to the British Museum but the project had fallen through because of 'the tactless and ungracious way in which you were received by the Director (Sir John Forsdyke)'. Since Sir John was now resigning, the Archbishop suggested that Beatty might reconsider the matter.

This rather extraordinary letter from the most important Principal Trustee of the British Museum, criticising the Director of that institution, caught Chester Beatty in an awkward position. It was quite true that he disliked Sir John Forsdyke who, though an excellent organiser (having supervised the evacuation of the British Museum collections during the Second World War), was a rather officious and pompous man. It was characteristic of Forsdyke that he asked that his retirement portrait should show him in full court dress.[66] Wilkinson wrote to Beatty enclosing a cutting from *The Times* which requested subscriptions to pay for Forsdyke's portrait. With thinly-veiled irony, Wilkinson noted: 'I am sure you will be hastening to contribute'.[67] But Beatty did not wish to explain the real reason for his displeasure with Forsdyke — the trouble over his Armenian manuscripts. He was not sure how he should answer the Archbishop's letter or if he should answer it at all.

Wilkinson cautioned him: 'We must bear in mind that an application to the Board of Trade by the Keeper of the Department of Manuscripts of the BM might lead to a rescinding of the licence to export'. In a postscript he added: 'Please don't let me know your final decision till I can get the Museum Papyri away'.[68] These papyri, which had been on loan to the British Museum, were collected by Wilkinson the following week.

Beatty consulted with his son, with Wilkinson and with his two London secretaries, John Wooderson and Jean Marsh, before replying to the Archbishop. They favoured an understated letter but Beatty decided to adopt a more direct approach, diplomatic yet pungent. He wrote:

> I thank you for your letter and I quite agree with your remarks about Sir John Forsdyke. Shortly before I attended a dinner at which he was also a guest, a certain person had made a very important gift to the British Museum, and when Sir John spoke at the dinner about this gift he showed no appreciation but gave the impression that it was a great privilege and honour to be allowed to present anything to the Museum. One of the other guests present spoke to me after the dinner and said, "Well, if that is their attitude I would rather throw my collections into the Thames than give them to the British Museum". There is no doubt that Sir John's manner was stupid, and if I had been contemplating giving anything to the Museum at that time, under no conditions whatsoever would I have done so while he was Director.[69]

It can be concluded that Beatty had not offered his collection to the British Museum as he was reputed to have done. Instead, it is possible that he hinted that he might be willing to part with some of his collections.

It is very difficult to believe, given the awkward affair regarding the Armenian manuscripts and Beatty's assertion that he wished to have nothing further to do with the British Museum, that Beatty would ever have offered his entire library to Sir John Forsdyke. Beatty ended his letter to the Archbishop by explaining that he was moving to Dublin where he hoped to establish a library which would be available to scholars as in the past:

Probably before I die I may decide definitely what to do with it, or I may leave the matter to my executors. I would like to say, however, how very much I appreciate your frank and friendly letter and to thank you for writing in this strain.

In a brief but courteous reply, the obviously disappointed Archbishop wrote: 'May I say how grateful I am for your kindly reply to my letter. I felt very anxious about writing and your reply has put my mind at rest'.[70]

This exchange of letters demonstrates the concern of people in positions of responsibility in cultural institutions in Great Britain about the decision of a generous benefactor like Chester Beatty to leave the country. For many, it must have been a sad reflection on the state of affairs under the Labour Party Government. Indeed Beatty showed his determination to leave Great Britain by instructing Wilkinson to cable him as soon as the biblical papyri arrived in Dublin. He did not intend to post his reply to the Archbishop until they were safely in Miller & Beatty's warehouse.[71]

On 15 January 1950, the last of the Chester Beatty Library was put on board an Aer Lingus flight for Dublin.[72] Later in the month, Wilkinson and his wife flew to Dublin with John Wooderson and Jean Marsh to spend five days examining possible sites for a library and to prepare the way for Beatty's arrival the following May.

The Significance of Chester Beatty's Decision

It is tempting to draw too many conclusions about the significance of Beatty's decision to move from one country to another. Given that the two countries in question are Great Britain and the Republic of Ireland, one might assume an Anglo-Irish dimension to the matter. But there is no evidence that Beatty intended to snub Great Britain by choosing to leave and it is unlikely that he gave much thought to the impact of his decision in political terms. Nonetheless, there are a number of aspects arising from his decision which deserve consideration.

Beatty was not alone in moving to the Republic of Ireland in the so-called 'Retreat from Moscow'. There had been considerable movement as a result of the Second World War, because Irish neutrality allowed relative comfort for some of the wealthy Britons who rented hotel rooms in Dublin or bought houses along the east coast. The registers of the Shelbourne Hotel in Dublin during the war years read at times like a roll-call of double-barrelled names of the British landed gentry. [73] After the war, most of these people returned to Great Britain but Ireland remained an attractive weekend retreat. Country estates were acquired, mainly in Counties Wicklow and Kildare, within easy reach of Dublin. Some estates were resold (like Chester Beatty Junior's 'Mount Armstrong') when the Conservative Party regained power in Great Britain in 1951. It was against this trend that Beatty moved to Ireland and declared: 'I intend to live and die in Dublin, which is the only place I know where one can find sanity and contented people'.[74]

This comment reflects Beatty's liking for the conservative nature of Irish life. He was, however, a rich man in a poor country. He may have admired Ireland because it was like Great Britain before the war, but the Ireland of the 1950s was economically depressed and suffering emigration on a terrifying scale. In the years 1946 to 1951 there was net emigration of 119,568 people, but the intercensal period showed a net increase for the first time since 1841.[75] By 1951 the tide had turned and emigration soared.

In 1962 Beatty said that he had 'confidence in Ireland of the future as a good place for young men to make their careers'.[76] The statistics show a sharp contrast as in the previous ten years, from 1951 to 1961, there had been net emigration of 412,404 people.[77] Irish political leaders appreciated that Beatty was willing to put faith in the country at a time when many had lost all hope. He brought a note of optimism which was sorely needed — a wealthy grand old gentleman who came to Ireland emphasising the importance of culture. He created few new jobs, built no factories and did not invest in Irish industry. Instead, he pursued an active retirement which was to symbolise hope for a better future — the day when people would have the education and leisure to appreciate a collection of art treasures from distant lands.

The Irish Government certainly understood Beatty's compliment when he said that Ireland was 'the freest country in the world'.[78] Implicit in his disapproval of the Labour Party Government in Great Britain, with its bureaucracy, regimentation and controls was an approval of the situation in Ireland. Beatty commented: 'I would prefer to spend my money on a bottle of stout in my garden in Dublin than on fountain-pen ink for filling up official forms in London'.[79] This was gentle diplomacy to indicate the kind of co-operation which Beatty expected in return for his promises to make cultural gifts to the Irish nation. There was official interest in Beatty from the day he spoke to Frederick Boland. Popular interest was proportionately significant. Beatty has no rivals in the period from 1950 to 1968 when Irish newspapers made him a focus of attention, the subject of over 250 articles.

Beatty could not have chosen a better moment to settle in Ireland. The Taoiseach, John A. Costello, announced the commissioning of the Bodkin Report with the words: 'While we are concentrating on our material advancement we should not, I think, neglect matters of the spirit . . . We have in this country great treasures of art. They are not sufficiently recognised or appreciated by our own people.'[80] Bodkin hoped that private individuals would come forward with support for the arts. In April 1951 Mr Costello was able to tell the Dáil of the Chester Beatty Gift to the National Gallery of Ireland:

> If we show in the future more interest in art . . . it may be that people like him will feel that we are deserving of encouragement and support, and that we may get more voluntary gifts of that kind further to enrich our artistic heritage here in Ireland.[81]

As Beatty's relationship with Ireland developed, Mr Costello's wish was to be more than adequately fulfilled.

Chapter 4

Gifts and Honour Abound

Mr Beatty is a person of considerable wealth and obviously benevolent intentions . . . On general grounds, therefore, he is a person worth encouraging.

Frederick H. Boland

Grande Entrée

Chester Beatty's involvement in Ireland can be seen on two levels — those of self-interest and public interest. While this dichotomy is difficult to state categorically, it can be said that, given Beatty's experience in the tough world of mining, his shrewd intelligence and his great wealth, his actions in the public interest were never likely to work to his personal detriment. In Ireland he hoped that these actions would secure him a pleasant retirement. There is no doubt that Beatty enjoyed flattery but it had to be carefully applied. Brendan Bracken wrote descriptively to Lord Beaverbrook about the need to raise money to improve the National Gallery in London:

I shall have a go at Chester Beatty. One of the best ways of getting some donations to your gallery from him would be for you to have him to lunch or dinner. He lives at Nice and so when you next go to the South of France have the old boy to lunch and give him what he, and I suppose all of us, like, lots of flattery. But don't lay it on with a trowel, as Disraeli said in advising ministers how to deal with Queen Victoria — in the Beatty case, lay it on with a crane.[1]

The National Gallery of Ireland did not need to ask for assistance from Beatty. In June 1949 he had told Frederick Boland of his intention to present a collection of French nineteenth-century paintings to the Irish Nation. The initial arrangements were made with Dr George Furlong (Director of the National Gallery of Ireland, 1935-50), and he recommended that the Board of Governors and Guardians of the Gallery should accept the gift.

It is clear that Beatty was keen to endear himself to the Irish authorities. Since he had no personal friends in the country, he had to introduce himself to Irish society. The gift of paintings was therefore a calculated element in an elaborate *grande entrée*. But while Beatty wished to prepare for his arrival in Dublin, he did not wish to excite the authorities in Great Britain. L.T. McCauley of the Department of External Affairs wrote to Dr Furlong to explain Beatty's position:

> Mr Beatty is anxious that the offer of his pictures to the Gallery should be treated as confidential. I understood him to say that permission for their export from England had been given but that the permit could be revoked at any time before export had taken place. If his offer became generally known, objections might be raised and the English authorities might be constrained to revoke the permit.[2]

The Irish authorities determined to help Beatty. McCauley contacted the Revenue Commissioners and arranged that, to avoid delay, the crates of pictures would be allowed through the Customs without being opened. The Revenue Commissioners further assisted matters when they advised that Customs duty would be waived as they would consider the pictures as being part of Mr Beatty's personal effects.[3] In the spring of 1950 the paintings were catalogued and an exhibition was organised for the following July.

Meanwhile a Dublin architect, Ian Roberts of McDonnell & Dixon, Architects, had been brought to London to see the library facilities at Baroda House. Beatty wished to have the magnificent Chinese ceiling of the Baroda Library incorporated in the design for a new library in Dublin. (Plate 17). This was to cause quite a headache for Roberts. The first building in Dublin which he proposed as a possible site for a library, 24 Earlsfort Terrace, was rejected by Beatty because the room most suitable for the Chinese ceiling was four feet too wide.

The next site to be considered was at 60 Fitzwilliam Square. Wilkinson thought the building 'would make into an ideal home for the collections'[4] and he was most disappointed when Roberts reported severe dry rot, damp and danger due to fire. Beatty consoled his librarian:

All these houses are, in my opinion, superficially very attractive for conversion into a Library, the elevations are charming, the rooms have fine mantelpieces but they are not well built and all have a tendency to dry rot. I think the next step is to try and find a house not quite so far out from Ailesbury Road and, if possible, detached . . . if it were a little way out from the centre of the City the air would be much better and there would be less smoke and dirt.[5]

In May 1950 Beatty moved into 10 Ailesbury Road, which had been completely refurbished. The following month he purchased a site at 20 Shrewsbury Road, just around the corner from Ailesbury Road, and he asked Roberts to draw up plans for a new purpose-built library.[6] The plans were prepared within a few weeks and forwarded to the Dublin City Manager's Office for approval. By late July Beatty had not received a favourable response and he became impatient. He decided to telephone Frederick Boland about the matter. Unfortunately Boland had gone to Strasbourg earlier in the day but his secretary forwarded Beatty's message:

Mr Beatty was wondering whether a word from you to the effect that there is official interest in the matter being expedited would be effective — he thinks it would be and would be most grateful if you could do anything.[7]

Boland instructed his secretary to write to Dr Nicholas George Nolan, Assistant Secretary at the Department of the Taoiseach, advising him:

17. Chinese ceiling and eighteenth century lantern, Chester Beatty Library, Dublin (formerly in Baroda House, London).

This Museum is intended to house his [Beatty's] priceless collection of Oriental MSS., generally considered to be one of the most important in the world. Various efforts have been made by private collectors and by Public Museums and Universities to acquire part or all of this collection, but Mr Beatty decided in favour of locating the whole collection in Dublin, and he intends that the public may have opportunities, from time to time, of viewing sections of it . . . It appears that the housing of the collection in a Museum in Dublin would undoubtedly be of great national benefit . . . we should accede to Mr Beatty's personal request to express our official interest in the building of this Museum to the Town Planning authorities with a view to having their approval of the plans expedited.[8]

Nolan acted on Boland's advice and on 4 August Beatty received news that the plans for his Museum had been approved. He wrote to Nolan: 'I am very much obliged for the promptness with which this matter has been dealt'.[9] He also wrote delightedly to Boland:

Thank you so much for all the trouble you took over the plans for my proposed building at Shrewsbury Road. I have just received a nice letter from the Assistant Secretary to the Taoiseach and have just heard that everything has been satisfactorily arranged.[10]

It is important to note that 'official interest' in Chester Beatty came at first from within the upper echelons of the Irish civil service. Once men like Boland and Nolan were convinced of Beatty's importance it was not long before the politicians in Government were also adopting a policy of enthusiastic welcome.

The Government was impressed by Beatty's gift of 93 paintings of the Barbizon and contemporary schools.[11] The gift to the nation was officially announced in July 1950 and the Government asked Mr Costello to convey 'an expression of their deep appreciation'.[12] The Taoiseach wrote to Beatty:

I hope to have the opportunity of meeting you soon and of expressing to you personally our sincere appreciation of your generous and public-spirited gesture, which I hope and believe that the Irish people, never unresponsive to such acts of kindness, will ever gratefully remember.[13]

Beatty replied: 'It is a great pleasure to me to present my collection of Barbizon pictures to the nation and I hope they give as much pleasure as I had in making the collection'.[14]

The Government decided to honour Chester Beatty by organising a grand opening of the exhibition of his pictures at the National Gallery of Ireland on 6 September, with a special dinner party afterwards. There were 220 invited guests at the exhibition opening and among those present were the Papal Nuncio, the American, Canadian and British Ambassadors, the two Archbishops of Dublin, the Tánaiste, eight Government Ministers, the Ceann Comhairle, the Cathaoirleach of the Seanad, the leader of the Opposition, the Lord Mayor of Dublin, T.D.s, and Senators.

The exhibition was opened by Mr Costello, who described the collection as 'one of the most magnificent benefactions connected with the Fine Arts which have ever been made to Ireland'.[15] (Plate 18).

18. *Presentation of Chester Beatty Collection to National Gallery of Ireland, 6 September 1950.*
L. to R.: Liam Cosgrave, A. Chester Beatty, John A. Costello (Taoiseach), Thomas McGreevy and Thomas Bodkin.

The Taoiseach took advantage of the occasion to announce his hopes for Irish cultural policy:

> We have still to establish our own national tradition in art. Such a tradition, the growth of which has been stunted by centuries of oppression and neglect, cannot be created by tariffs or quotas, still less by prohibitions on the import of artistic ideas. To the extent to which conditions wherein such growth may blossom and thrive can be fostered or created, it is the duty of the State and of statesmen to lend their aid.[16]

It would be easy to accuse Costello of hypocrisy given, for example, the rigid censorship laws, but the importance of this speech should not be underestimated. Beatty's arrival in Ireland coincided with the first sincere and determined attempt by the leader of an Irish government to formulate a policy with regard to the arts. Thomas Bodkin wrote to the Earl of Rosse: 'I have excellent reason to think that Mr Costello is deeply interested in the cause of art in Ireland, more so than any Irish statesman for the past fifty years'.[17]

Beatty was pleased with the exhibition opening but he especially enjoyed the dinner hosted by the Taoiseach at the Russell Hotel. It was a good opportunity for Beatty to meet distinguished members of Irish society and he appreciated Costello's thoughtfulness in organising the dinner: 'I would like to thank you for all your trouble and kindness to me and to tell you how much I enjoy living in Ireland and how happy I am here. The people are so kind and hospitable'.[18]

The art critics of 23 Irish newspapers, magazines and journals attended the opening of the 'Chester Beatty Collection'. In general, their opinion of the pictures was favourable but the opinion of the visiting public was not quite so appreciative. Bodkin wrote to Costello to tell him that he had been to see the exhibition 'and was immensely impressed by its merits and importance. Dublin opinion seems to be taking a most erroneous view of it'.[19]

The most antagonistic review appeared in *The Leader*. The art critic Patrick W. Hickey wrote:

> I must admit that I read some of the abuse — and heard a lot more — levelled at this latest acquisition by the

trustees – before I went to see for myself . . . Unfortunately, public opinion was right . . . Most of them are plainly absolute rubbish and should have been refused.[20]

The artist Seán Keating commented on this type of ignorant art criticism: 'In Dublin the qualification for a critic seems to be that he should have made a mess of the football news'.[21]

Beatty knew that Irish attitudes to art were not overly-sophisticated. He thought that the only way to improve the response to art was by exposing people to it. He advised the Government that some of his pictures should be distributed on loan to various regional centres. A suitable scheme was organised by Thomas McGreevy and Dr Nolan of the Department of the Taoiseach.[22]

Whatever public opinion of Beatty's pictures may have been, his personality excited widespread interest. The story of 'the copper millionaire and world-famous collector'[23] was a romantic one and ideal material for feature articles in newspapers. Beatty's good humour and his positive comments found favour with Irish journalists: 'I am not worrying about being happy here; I love the country and what more matters'.[24] In an enthusiastic response, the *Evening Herald* claimed that Beatty's father and grandfather were born in Dublin.[25] Although this was quite untrue, Beatty never formally denied the story and it was repeated many times over the next 18 years.[26] Perhaps he felt flattered but he must have been surprised when the *Irish Independent*, in a final act of appropriation, published a story with the headline 'His Father Was Born In Dublin'.[27]

Beatty did not intend to be in Dublin for 12 months of each year. He hoped to spend 4 months in the city, from May to September, living for the rest of the year in the South of France. He joked that he could never survive an Irish winter and preferred the warmth of the Riviera. However, he gave some validity to rumours about his Irish ancestry when, in an effort to reorganise his financial affairs, he purchased a burial plot at Glasnevin Cemetery, Dublin, on 22 September 1950.[28] This was a novel method of attempting to establish domicile in Ireland, since it indicated that Beatty intended to reside in the country even though he would be absent at times. He thus persuaded the Government of his sincerity and also availed of the tax advantages of being an Irish resident.

Beatty appreciated the willingness of the Irish authorities to make special provision for him. He found the Irish attitude to his need for foreign currency particularly refreshing. One documented instance illustrates the extent to which Beatty was facilitated in this regard.

Before he left for the South of France in October 1950, Beatty applied for French francs by sending medical certificates to the Department of External Affairs, stating that he suffered from silicosis of the left lung and that his doctors advised that he should spend the winter in a warm climate. Beatty was grateful to Boland, who agreed to attend to the administrative details: 'It is very kind of you to take so much trouble about my health allowance'.[29]

The Irish authorities recognised that a man of Beatty's wealth needed a very considerable sum of foreign currency to maintain his lifestyle and to purchase material for his art collections. On 5 September Boland wrote to J.J. McElligott, Secretary of the Department of Finance, enclosing a list of Beatty's holdings of French stocks and shares valued by the Bourse in Paris at over 25,000,000 francs. Boland wrote:

> Chester Beatty is anxious to sell five or ten thousand pounds worth of the shares. We are telling him to make an application . . . and we hope that it will be possible for you to grant it when it comes along.[30]

McElligott replied to Boland that he had permitted the Bank of Ireland to sell 'sufficient of the securities to realise £10,000 approximately, the proceeds to be lodged in a bank at Nice where Chester Beatty intends to spend the winter'.[31] As an additional gesture, the Department of Finance authorised that Beatty be given traveller's cheques to the value of £2,500.[32] It is little wonder that Beatty found the workings of Irish bureaucracy more attractive than the rigid regulations which he had encountered in Great Britain under the Labour Party Government.

The following month Beatty was again alarmed by the British authorities when he received a letter from the Secretary of the Committee on the Export of Works of Art, asking for his opinion on proposed government policy.[33] Beatty felt that the British Government was planning to recall his collections, especially the biblical papyri. Wilkinson gently advised him:

> We must understand the Government's point of view — they have to consider the financial as well as the cultural loss. Unfortunately this involves interfering with the liberty of people to control their private property. Should the Elgin Marbles be returned to Greece and the National Gallery go back to Italy, France, etc?[34]

Beatty would probably have preferred to ignore Wilkinson's last sentence as if the logic were applied to his own collections the consequences would have been severe.

In his reply to the Committee, Beatty offered two main arguments. Firstly, he suggested that the Committee's main purpose should be the protection 'of English works of art but also would cover other works of art if they were considered of very great importance to the country'.[35] This was a little disingenuous, as his own biblical papyri were without doubt items of very great importance. Secondly, Beatty argued that the public collections of England were superb and the problem was the lack of exhibition space for some of the best items. Beatty's tongue-in-cheek solution to the matter was for the British Government to encourage a more liberal policy regarding the export of art works! London would not retain her position as the centre of art dealing if the rules for export were inflexible. The Committee must have been surprised at the brazen nature of Beatty's reply but he heard no more from the authorities in Great Britain.

Quite the opposite was true in Ireland. Beatty received confirmation of the success of his *grande entrée* when, a few weeks after leaving for the South of France, he was informed that both Dublin University and the National University of Ireland wished to award him honorary degrees.

Dublin University decided to honour Beatty when the Provost of Trinity College, Dr Ernest H. Alton, revealed that some of the famous Chester Beatty biblical papyri would be displayed on loan at the College Library. Wilkinson took care of the necessary arrangements and the exhibition was opened in December.[36] Beatty was conferred with an Honorary

Doctor of Laws on 5 July 1951.[37] A week later, on 12 July, he received a similar degree from Eamon de Valera, Chancellor of the National University of Ireland.[38] Rt Rev Mgr Edward Kissane, Pro-Vice Chancellor of the National University and President of St Patrick's College, Maynooth, had proposed that Beatty should be honoured 'in recognition of his practical assistance in providing facilities for the wider appreciation of art and literature'.[39]

The growth of Beatty's friendship with Mgr Kissane can be credited to Thomas McGreevy. When the guest list was being organised for the dinner after the opening of the Chester Beatty Exhibition at the National Gallery of Ireland, McGreevy had written to the Department of the Taoiseach with the shrewd suggestion that Mgr Kissane should be invited: 'I'd be surprised if, once he was on visiting terms at Maynooth, Mr Chester Beatty did not show a desire to be helpful wherever he could about the Library there'.[40]

McGreevy was not alone in possessing an acquisitive impulse. Beatty seemed to attract admirers like bees around a honey-pot. Dr Farrington, Secretary of the Royal Irish Academy, wrote to Dr Alton with the suggestion that Beatty might like to become an honorary member of the Academy.[41] Dr Alton agreed to propose Beatty after gaining his approval and he was elected to membership on 30 November 1951.[42] This was the extent of Beatty's participation, as there is no record of his having attended a meeting of the Academy and he did not present any gifts.

On 4 December 1951, Beatty was honoured once again with the announcement that he had been appointed an ordinary member of the first Arts Council.[43] It had at first been proposed that the members of the Arts Council should be specialists and should have a particular interest in the Irish language. After the fall of the Inter-Party Government, the incoming Taoiseach, Eamon de Valera, decided to take the advice of P.J. Little, T.D., to appoint as members only those with a real feeling for cultural interests, 'a broad mature outlook and a certain standing to give authority to decisions and guiding general policy'.[44] De Valera felt that Beatty was such a person and proposed him for membership.[45] Beatty was delighted and wrote to the Taoiseach: 'Anything I can do when I am in Ireland – or anything I can do when I am away from Ireland – it will be a great pleasure to do'.[46]

Beatty remained a member of the Arts Council until 1962, when he resigned 'on grounds of age'.[47] His presence on the Council gave 'a certain standing' to decisions made but he did not attend meetings very often.[48]

In September 1953 he presented the Council with a Film Recording Unit, consisting of two projectors, screen and sound equipment. He instructed that the equipment should be used 'to spread the knowledge and promote the practice of the Arts'.[49] This was the task which he had set himself during his retirement years in Ireland.

Patron of the Arts

Beatty's enthusiastic promotion of the arts was most obvious in his approach to the organisation of his Library. This was his main preoccupation and it produced voluminous correspondence – two or three letters a day for 15 years. Without doubt, Beatty hoped to perpetuate his name by creating a splendid memorial in Dublin. To complete this task he depended on the ability of his staff. He employed a Dublin lady, Joan O'Neill, as his business secretary. The burden of the organisation of the Chester Beatty Library fell on the shoulders of James Wilkinson.

Despite the efforts which had been made to expedite planning approval for the Library, the building took longer to complete than anticipated. Beatty decided to provide a residence for Wilkinson within the Library grounds. In April 1952 Wilkinson and his wife moved to Dublin.[50] They were followed by Wilfred Merton, Beatty's friend and book publisher, who had purchased a house on the Stillorgan Road not far from the Library.[51] Beatty's bank manager James Hosking[52] and his book restorer Ida Dyson[53] also followed him to Dublin.

Wilkinson found the experience of living in Dublin very difficult. He decided to read some books about Ireland but he had little interest in the country.[54] When a friend asked him to recommend accommodation in Kerry, he candidly admitted: 'I have never left Dublin except for short drives'.[55]

This was also true of Beatty but he had, perhaps, more of an excuse given his age.

In June 1952 Beatty pursued his attempt to attract 'official interest' in his Library. He visited Frederick Boland (who had been posted to London as Irish Ambassador) to ask him if the Taoiseach, Mr de Valera, would like to come to see the building. Unfortunately the visit was delayed due to the death of Beatty's wife, Edith. Boland sent Beatty a message of sympathy on behalf of the Government.[56] The Taoiseach informed Beatty that he would be pleased to attend the opening of the Library when it had been arranged.[57]

The following year, on 8 August, the Chester Beatty Library was officially opened at a ceremony in the Library grounds. (Plate 19). Beatty formally opened the private Library but the attendance included the Taoiseach, the Minister for Finance (Seán MacEntee), the Minister for External Affairs (Frank Aiken), Frederick Boland and Mgr Kissane. Mr de Valera spent an hour examining the exhibits and in a short address he said:

19. The Chester Beatty Library, Dublin, 1953.

We have here, for scholars to examine, some of the oldest records of human ingenuity on the one hand, and of culture on the other. Thanks to Mr Beatty, this library will be a mecca for scholars for generations to come. We thank him for his hospitality and our appreciation for making our country such a centre.[58]

On 25 September the newspapers announced 'Another Beatty Gift to Nation'.[59] Beatty had presented a valuable collection of 143 items of rare Oriental weaponry to the Minister for Defence, Oscar Traynor.[60] The gift would be displayed at the Curragh Camp Military College Museum. Beatty told the guests at the presentation ceremony:

I cannot tell you now much I have enjoyed living in Ireland during the last two years and I hope to finish my days here . . . Ireland is a country on the threshold of a great future.[61]

Beatty did not confine his optimism to his public statements. He would often write private letters encouraging people to visit Dublin, which he thought 'a very attractive city' with 'a rather delightful summer climate'.[62]

He wrote to the Attorney General, Patrick McGilligan:

It would greatly help in strengthening Ireland's economic position if more were done to attract to the country individuals of substance, successful businessmen and retired people, particularly from the United Kingdom and from the British Commonwealth. In addition to attracting people to settle permanently in Ireland, it would further contribute to the trade and development of the country if individuals were encouraged to own property in Ireland and spend part of their leisure time there.

An influx of immigrants and resident visitors . . . would be likely to help Ireland financially. It would, by hypothesis, bring into the country people of ability and in some cases of leisure and of culture, and many of these would certainly come to play an important part in the future development of the country.[63]

Beatty became a member of the Friends of the National Collections of Ireland[64] but he felt that there was scope for a more ambitious scheme of art patronage. He had told Boland of his wish to establish an Irish-American Foundation.[65] He wrote to Thomas McGreevy:

> There are about 40 million people of Irish descent in America and I feel that is a great source of capital which we must somehow or other tap. Ireland is a wonderful country, with wonderful people, and we must somehow or other make Dublin a great art centre and cultural centre of Europe. Look how Munich developed before the war ... it will awaken an enormous amount of interest in people of Irish descent ... if this could be developed in the next five or ten years, I feel it could help towards the prosperity of Ireland.[66]

Beatty contacted Thomas Bodkin and they discussed the matter. Beatty admired Bodkin's *Report on the Arts* and felt that he should encourage any government initiative. He had supported the National Art Collections Fund in Great Britain and he wrote to the President, Sir Robert Witt, for his advice. Witt could not foresee a generous response in Ireland because there were too few moneyed people to support the scheme.[67] Beatty began to realise that he would have to adapt his ideas to suit the Irish situation. His library of Oriental art contained 'the cream of the rare texts from the East' but Beatty noted: 'Eastern things are regarded as rather out of the way'.[68] The Irish public could not appreciate the Chester Beatty Library until they had first been encouraged to treasure their own heritage.

Bord Fáilte (The Irish Tourist Board) had come to the same conclusion and in 1953 a cultural festival was organised. Under the title of 'An Tóstal' (the Pageant), various cultural activities took place throughout the country from 5 to 26 April. Beatty was particularly impressed by an exhibition of Irish manuscripts at Trinity College Library.[69]

There was mixed reaction to 'An Tóstal' among the general public. An editorial in the *Evening Herald* stated that the festival was a noble gesture but 'it was obvious that the amount spent abroad on advertising was greater than the total receipts from foreign visitors'.[70] The Taoiseach, Mr de Valera, argued:

> An Tóstal has given our people a feeling of what can be secured by co-operation. It has thrown us back largely on ourselves, making us think of the things of the past and realising the treasures we really possess ... An Tóstal is going to be very far from the stunt some people regarded it at the start. It will be something of value both in the material and spiritual sense.[71]

For the next few years Beatty supported the efforts of the organisers of 'An Tóstal' by arranging special exhibitions and opening his Library to the public for the duration of the festival. He also began to include among the purchases for the Library, items which would appeal to an Irish audience. He admired Irish eighteenth-century bookbinding and he found that fine bindings were 'decidedly cheap'.[72] (Plate 20). He instructed Wilkinson to notify him of the sale of old maps, engravings and printed books of specific Irish interest.[73] Wilfred Merton was asked to examine the sale catalogues for rare books written by Jesuit missionaries to the East (usually called Jesuit Relations). Beatty wrote: 'I want to concentrate on the Jesuit books, which is very important in a Catholic country like Ireland'.[74]

While in Ireland Beatty became interested in the Catholic religion. He did not practise any formal religion because he could not tolerate dogma[75] or the routine of regular mass-going.[76] His wife Edith was a practising Catholic. She had an Irish chaplain for many years, Fr King, SJ., who said mass for her in a private chapel which had been built at Beatty's country residence at Calehill Park in Kent. After Mrs Beatty's death in 1952, Fr King was transferred to the Jesuit House in Dublin, Milltown Park. Beatty met him on a number of occasions but he decided that Catholic theology was complex and he was too old to discuss it. His main concern was not religion but the organisation of his Library.

Beatty wanted the Library building to be a showpiece of Irish craftsmanship. He insisted on the use of Irish materials — Connemara marble in the entrance hall, oak parquet floors, and solid mahogany exhibition cases. But soon after the

20. An Irish bookbinding, c. 1760
(courtesy Trustees of the CBL).

Library was opened in August 1953 Beatty decided that it was inadequate. He needed more exhibition space. The Library had been built with the idea of adding another storey if this was necessary. On investigation Beatty found that it would be less

81

expensive to build a new gallery beside the existing one. He was developing a policy which would guarantee the future of the Library after his death. The policy depended on whether or not the Irish public could be encouraged to visit 20 Shrewsbury Road.

Public interest in the Chester Beatty Library was enhanced in the summer of 1954. Queen Elizabeth II's Birthday Honours List, published on 10 June, announced that Alfred Chester Beatty had been made a Knight Bachelor.[77] It is said that Churchill had promised to honour Beatty after the Allied victory in 1945. The Conservative Party's defeat in the General Election delayed the matter. After Churchill returned to power he was reminded of his promise and he proposed Beatty for a knighthood. The investiture took place at Buckingham Palace on 6 July. The Irish newspapers took advantage of the occasion to recall Beatty's many gifts since his arrival in Dublin.[78]

Beatty took great pleasure in being addressed as 'Sir Chester'. Nothing pleased him more, however, than the interest of scholars and the general public in his art collections. He decided to open his Library to the public and he asked Mr de Valera if he would perform the official ceremony. The Taoiseach agreed and the opening took place on 11 August. (Plate 21). In an amusing effort to endear himself to his Irish audience, Beatty adopted de Valera's habit of introducing and closing his speech with a phrase in the Irish language. He enthused:

> Dublin is a city of wonderful culture and art consciousness. Ireland has a great art tradition. I hope that the opening of this library will encourage it, especially among the growing generation.[79]

The Arts Council decided to make a special gesture in appreciation of Beatty's munificence as a patron of the arts. The artist Seán O'Sullivan was commissioned to paint his portrait.[80] The painting was presented to Beatty on 30 September by John A. Costello, who had just been made Taoiseach for the second time.[81]

It did not matter to Beatty if the Taoiseach happened to be Costello or de Valera. He did not wish to be identified with

*21. Opening of the Chester Beatty Library to the Public, 11
August 1954. L. to R.: Mgr. Edward Kissane, Eamon de Valera
(Taoiseach), Fr. Senan OFM Cap., A. Chester Beatty.*

a political party in Ireland. Whereas in Great Britain he was
strongly identified with the Conservative Party, he found
little difference between the two major Irish political parties,
Fianna Fáil and Fine Gael. He only expressed an opinion on a
political matter on one occasion. He became interested in the
Lane pictures controversy.[82] His interest arose because he
saw the case as a cultural matter and his opinion about it was
expressed privately.

The campaign for the return of the Lane pictures had been
the most actively pursued element of cultural politics for some
20 years. At the opening of the Chester Beatty Collection at
the National Gallery of Ireland in September 1950, Costello
declared:

> These new and splendid possessions which we take over
> today should inspire us, accordingly, to continue unfal-
> teringly the long campaign for the restoration of the
> Lane pictures to Dublin, for which Sir Hugh Lane des-
> tined them and where there is now better reason than
> ever for their presence.[83]

Bodkin and McGreevy explained the merits of the Irish case to Beatty. He was convinced: 'The fact is really that the pictures belong legally to England and morally to Ireland, and the only solution is a compromise'.[84]

He wrote to Costello that Ireland should argue for a loan rather than possession of the pictures. After they had been on loan to Dublin for a number of years it would be easier to claim possession. Beatty advised:

> One has to look at the matter from a business standpoint and you, as a practical man with a great deal of experience in business, will know very well that in the business world one can very rarely get 100% of what one wants.[85]

In 1959 a compromise agreement was made along the lines suggested by Beatty.[86]

The warm friendship between Beatty and McGreevy was of great benefit to the National Gallery of Ireland. Beatty wrote: 'The National Gallery of Ireland is not at all appreciated, as it is fantastically fine, and considering the size of the city, quite an unusual collection'.[87] Punning on the name of a common pain-relieving tablet (May and Baker's product), he joked that 'old M & B' (McGreevy and Beatty) would solve the Gallery's problems.

Following the gift of French nineteenth-century paintings, Beatty presented the National Gallery with 48 paintings,[88] 253 drawings and miniatures,[89] and 6 sculptures.[90] Needless to say, the scale of Beatty's gifts makes him one of the most generous benefactors of the Gallery.

Beatty allowed McGreevy the liberty to choose whether or not to exhibit the items which he presented. He wrote:

> I do not want simply to offer things to the Gallery and have them accepted because you do not want to turn me down. I want to do everything I can to build up the Gallery, and if I offer anything which is not of the proper quality I hope you will be perfectly frank and turn it down immediately.[91]

Many paintings were indeed consigned to the cellars but others were proudly displayed as important additions to the national collections. McGreevy was very grateful for these gifts.

Beatty was to disappoint him, however, regarding a promise to give the Gallery a collection of Impressionist and Post-Impressionist paintings as a memorial to his wife. In December 1952 Beatty wrote a long letter to McGreevy.[92] Edith Beatty had died intestate and under British law she was therefore considered to have held the domicile of her husband. A complicated legal tangle developed, much to Beatty's frustration. Under the arrangement between Great Britain and the Republic of Ireland, his wife's property in England was subject to English death duties. However, the bulk of her furniture, pictures, manuscripts and porcelain were considered to be of national importance and were declared free of death duties until they were sold. Beatty hoped that an arrangement could be made between the British and Irish authorities. He hoped that the Irish Government would declare the same articles to be of national importance. With the support of the Irish authorities, Beatty would then apply for permission to move the articles to Ireland with the proviso that if he should sell them the death duties would be paid to the British Government.

McGreevy was excited by the prospect of acquiring one of the best private collections in Europe. Throughout 1953 negotiations took place until in January 1954 Beatty reported: 'I am going to give you some pictures in the coming year or so, and among them I believe there are two Monets and also a superb Pissarro'.[93] He had just discovered a law by which pictures over 100 years old could be exported to the sterling area. In September the British Board of Trade granted Beatty's request to exhibit the paintings on loan in Dublin and an exhibition was opened at the National Gallery of Ireland.[94] Beatty informed McGreevy:

As you know, it is my hope to be in a position to give or bequeath to the National Gallery of Ireland a representative selection of the pictures from my wife's collection . . . I may say that I hope that most of the pictures in the present loan will ultimately go to the Gallery as a memorial to my wife. And as an earnest of that hope and intention I herewith offer the Cézanne watercolour view of the Montagne Ste Victoire as a gift.[95]

A press release prepared by the Gallery to announce the

exhibition gently asserted: 'The present loan is in the nature of a harbinger of things to come'.[96]

Unfortunately for the National Gallery, Beatty's enthusiasm had got the better of him. He had not given sufficient consideration to the need to pay death duties at the rate of 65% on his wife's estate. This was to be a severe financial blow and Beatty decided that the only way he could pay the duty was to sell the Impressionist paintings.

It was not necessary to sell all the paintings immediately, as the collection was a large one. In November 1956 Beatty gave another eight paintings on loan to the National Gallery. They were withdrawn in May 1957[97] and four more paintings were withdrawn in June 1959. Beatty apologised to McGreevy:

> I am sorry I have not got an unlimited number, because if I had a big collection left I would be glad to give the Gallery some Impressionists in addition to the Cézanne watercolour that I gave them.[98]

The British Government agreed to waive death duties on much of Edith Beatty's estate if those articles which were of national importance were sold to galleries in Great Britain. While McGreevy understood Beatty's position, he must have found it difficult to sit back calmly as British provincial galleries acquired the paintings which had been promised to the National Gallery of Ireland.

In March 1962 McGreevy had what at first seemed to be a brainwave. He wrote to Dudley Tooth of Messrs Arthur Tooth & Sons of London, who were handling the sale of Beatty's pictures.[99] He suggested that the legal position regarding Commonwealth galleries might still include those in Ireland. If this was the case, Beatty's pictures could be sold to Irish galleries without liability for death duty. Tooth replied: 'I think Sir Chester knows himself that the National Gallery of Ireland does not come under the scheme . . . I wish I could help but it seems that nothing can be done'.[100]

McGreevy decided to write to Seán Réamonn, Chairman of the Irish Revenue Commissioners, to make certain that Tooth was correct. Réamonn confirmed Tooth's opinion and McGreevy pursued the matter no further.[101]

Beatty had found it necessary to put self-interest before

public interest but it would be wrong to place emphasis on the affair. The paintings were sold to British galleries where they could be viewed by the general public. If in this instance the Irish people did not benefit from Beatty's munificence, there were other occasions throughout the 1950s when he made arrangements for their special benefit.

In 1955 Beatty firmly established himself as Ireland's foremost cultural benefactor. Two exhibitions were organised at Trinity College with material loaned from the Chester Beatty Collections.

Beatty had begun to collect Japanese wood-block prints the previous year and he suggested that they be exhibited during 'An Tóstal'. He wrote to the Earl of Rosse: 'It is simply a case of how keen they are in Ireland to have the Exhibition. If you think it would be a great success and they would be very anxious to have it, then I would be prepared to pay the expenses'.[102] He also asked the Earl of Rosse if an exhibition of Western illuminated manuscripts would be of interest. He was assured that the organising committee of 'An Tóstal' would be delighted to have both exhibitions.

The Irish President, Seán T. O'Kelly, agreed to open the 'Exhibition of Japanese Colour Prints' at the Regent House of Trinity College on 10 May.[103] (Plate 22). Beatty was pleased with the response to the exhibition. It was, in effect, the first time such a collection had been displayed in Dublin. President O'Kelly enthused that Thomas Davis had written of the place of art in a revivified nation and had deplored the lack of art in the Ireland of his day. The country owed sincere gratitude to Sir Chester Beatty who, through his initiative, was helping to satisfy the aesthetic needs of the new Ireland.[104]

A week later, on 18 May, the Rector of Lincoln College, Oxford, Walter Oakeshott, officially opened the 'Exhibition of Western Illuminated Manuscripts' at Trinity College Library.[105] The response was again favourable — Beatty's enthusiasm was infectious. It was difficult to believe that he was 80 years of age.

Beatty took advantage of the publicity surrounding the exhibitions at Trinity College to advertise the Library at Shrewsbury Road. Wilkinson arranged to have notices displayed at the National Museum, the National Library, the

Royal Dublin Society and Bord Fáilte tourist offices. The opening hours of the Chester Beatty Library were advertised in the national newspapers.

22. *Exhibition of Japanese Prints, Trinity College, Dublin, May 1955.*

The result was disappointing. Beatty would often go around to his Library on a Wednesday afternoon to meet the visitors only to find that none had arrived. He was disheartened at times but steadfastly refused to become pessimistic. He wrote fondly of the Library's 'little island site away from all noise and dirt'[106] but he was concerned about its position 'away from the centre of things in Dublin'.[107] Nevertheless, he continued to organise the building of an extension to the Library.

Throughout the 1950s Beatty purchased material for his collections. He hoped to have time 'to put the finishing touches to the Library' and joked: 'The doctors tell me I ought to make 100 years but I am not so anxious for that, because when one gets very, very old, life is not so interesting'.[108] He wrote to Wilkinson:

> In a few years I think we shall have improved the collection enormously, and probably it will be one of the best private collections in Europe. The great thing is not to try to make the collection too big ... I think our policy should be gradually to improve ... Quality, quality, always the quality.[109]

Many scholars were invited to Dublin, at Beatty's expense, to work at the Chester Beatty Library during the summer.[110] The fruits of their researches were then published in order to make the collections available to the widest possible audience.

Beatty greatly appreciated those who recognised the time, effort and money which he had invested in his art collections. He knew that leading Irish politicians and civil servants were willing to facilitate him. The Irish Customs authorities took a little longer to see the benefit of such co-operation. They were understandably unaware of the difficulties faced by an art collector like Beatty because they had not encountered anyone like him.

A problem arose in January 1955 when Beatty acquired a seventeenth-century wooden figure of an Oriental warrior. (Plate 23). He sent it to Dublin from Paris where he had bought it. To suit French Customs regulations the figure was declared to be less than 100 years old. Although this allowed the figure to leave France free of duty, it meant that it was subject to duty in Ireland. Wilkinson complained to Beatty:

> First of all I had to pay £11 for freight and now the Customs demand £30 for import duty. Anyhow I'm trying to get the Customs to let us off on the ground that your library is really a benefit to the people of Ireland, but I do not suppose they will be obliging. These Customs affairs are an intolerable nuisance.[111]

Beatty thought that the question of import duty was absurd:

> If we are going to buy things and bring them to Ireland we must have this matter settled. What is the point pay-

23. *Beatty experienced difficulty importing these two sculptures, a bronze Buddha (foreground) and a wooden oriental warrior (background) (courtesy of Trustees of the CBL).*

ing £40 for the figure if it costs £41 to get it to the Library at Shrewsbury Road? If I am going to keep buying things on a rising market, as there is on these things . . . it means that if they put these duties on I will have to stop buying . . . it is an old figure, it should go in free. America allows all antiques in free.[112]

Wilkinson wrote to the Department of Industry and Commerce but received no reply. Beatty asked his solicitor, Dermot McGillicuddy, to take up the matter. The Customs authorities informed McGillicuddy that they treated every case on its merits.[113] The wooden figure was allowed through free of duty but Beatty was unimpressed by the wrangle involved in having it admitted.

In May 1956 there was further difficulty regarding customs duty. A consignment of Japanese prints was deemed liable for duty. Beatty contacted the Attorney General, Patrick McGilligan, and asked him to prevent this problem from recurring. Every time Beatty attempted to import something free of duty, the Customs demanded a certificate of antiquity signed by a member of the Antique Dealers' Association (A.D.A.). Beatty requested that his librarian should be authorised to issue such a certificate although he was not a member of the A.D.A. The Revenue Commissioners ignored Beatty's request, although the prints in question were admitted free of duty.[114]

Beatty instructed Wilkinson to write a strongly-worded letter to the Revenue Commissioners. Politely but pointedly, Wilkinson argued:

> There are certain special reasons to justify a claim for exemption from duty in the case of articles purchased for this Library and I may, perhaps, add that if duty is to be charged on them, Sir Chester Beatty may be discouraged from importing objects for his various collections which he is really forming for the benefit of the people of Ireland.[115]

This time the message was given appropriate attention and Beatty had no further problems regarding customs duty.

The policy of 'official interest' in Chester Beatty operated at all levels of administration.[116] He was encouraged by the efforts made to accommodate him. The Irish authorities interpreted the establishment of the Chester Beatty Library in Dublin as a gesture of confidence in Ireland's future. Soon he was to receive the highest honours of both the city and the country of his adoption.

A 'Kissing of Hands'

Each year on 7 February, Beatty received a telegram from the Taoiseach wishing him many happy returns on his birthday. He received such greetings from John A. Costello, Eamon de Valera and Seán Lemass.[117] President O'Kelly also sent messages of congratulation. Beatty was flattered that they should bother and their consideration meant a lot to him. He had come to Ireland in the hope that he would be given the type of consideration which had been lacking in post-war Britain. Ireland still operated on the premise that every case was treated on its merits. Beatty's worthiness was never in doubt.

On 7 November 1955, a motion to honour Sir Chester Beatty as a Freeman of the City of Dublin was passed by a meeting of Dublin City Council.[118] Beatty was delighted with the honour but he was not sure what it meant. Wilkinson wrote to offer his congratulations: 'I read about it in an English paper, someone suggests that it gives you the privilege of driving on the other side of the road!'[119] Beatty was told that the Freedom of Dublin was a purely honorific and complimentary title.[120] He was impressed that he would only be the 44th person to receive the award.

The conferring ceremony took place on 26 July 1956 at the Mansion House. The distinguished gathering included President O'Kelly, John A. Costello, Eamon de Valera, Oscar Traynor, Seán MacEntee and Thomas McGreevy. The Lord Mayor, Robert Briscoe, presented Beatty with an illuminated certificate and, in his address, said:

It was right and proper . . . that the City Council, acting for and in the name of the people of Dublin, should have decided to mark their appreciation of Sir Alfred's benefactions and generosity by offering to confer on him the highest gift at their disposal — to make him an Honorary Freeman and Burgess of the City of Dublin.[121]

Beatty replied graciously:

> I feel very humble when I think of my great predecessors on the roll. I am very touched by what you have conferred on me and I will uphold the honour of this great city, which has done so much in spreading learning and civilisation throughout the world.[122]

The *Irish Independent* reacted to the award with a certain amount of vindication. It was logical that Beatty should become a Freeman of Dublin because his father and grandfather were natives of the city![123]

Later in 1956, Beatty told Seán T. O'Kelly that he wished to become an Irish citizen.[124] The President asked officials of the Departments of Justice and External Affairs to consider the matter. They advised that Beatty could be granted citizenship as a token honour under Section 12 of the Irish Nationality and Citizenship Act, 1956.[125] Beatty would be the first person to receive Honorary Citizenship under the new Act.[126]

Thomas Coyne, Secretary of the Department of Justice, wrote to his opposite number in the Taoiseach's Department, Maurice Moynihan, seeking the approval of the Government so that a certificate of naturalisation could be issued to Beatty.[127] Moynihan replied that he would ask the Government to consider that Beatty qualified for Honorary Citizenship because he had rendered 'distinguished service' to the nation. He suggested that 'the simplest, most expeditious and cheapest way' to arrange the matter was to have the award typed on vellum. Ideally, the award should be presented by the President but since Beatty was away in the South of France, Moynihan advised Coyne: 'the simplest thing would be for you to post it to him'.[128]

Coyne did not agree:

> It would be treating the grant of citizenship all too casually if the certificate were simply to be put in an envelope and posted to him. Sir Chester himself dearly loves show and panoply and I think that his regard for the token of honour will be enhanced if it is accompanied

by a "kissing of hands" with the President and exchanges of mutual esteem ... I think you should also consider what publicity might be given in the matter and whether press photographs may be taken of the certificate. I think that a certain amount of publicity of the right kind would be a good thing.[129]

The Government granted its approval and on 19 January 1957 a certificate of Honorary Irish Citizenship was signed by the President and Taoiseach.[130]

The 'kissing of hands' took place on 7 August when President O'Kelly presented the certificate to Beatty after a private luncheon at Áras an Uachtaráin. As Coyne had predicted, the presentation was accompanied by 'exchanges of mutual esteem'. Beatty called the occasion 'my proudest moment'.[131] President O'Kelly told the press corps:

Sir Alfred Chester Beatty is a citizen of the world — one of those of whom it may be said that his heart is no island cut off from other lands, but a continent that joins them together ... It is no wonder, then, that the public authorities of other countries have been delighted to honour him, and the people of Ireland, who have no less reason to be grateful for his benefactions, should wish to do so too.[132]

Press photographs reaffirmed Beatty's position as an officially approved patron of the arts in Ireland. (Plate 24).

A few weeks later, on 24 August, President and Mrs O'Kelly attended the official opening by the Taoiseach of the new gallery at the Chester Beatty Library. (Plates 25 and 26). There were over 200 guests and Mr de Valera addressed them:

Sir Chester Beatty has earned and receives the grateful appreciation of the people of Ireland and it is a pleasure to be able to greet him as a fellow citizen. From an Irish point of view, it is natural that visitors to this Library should be most interested in the illuminated manuscripts and the fine collection of Irish bindings. But visitors can also study Arabic texts, Persian paintings, manuscripts from India, Turkey, China and Japan ... When visitors have seen the exhibits on display they should realise

24. *First Honorary Irish Citizen — 7 August 1957. L. to R.: Eamon de Valera (Taoiseach), Seán T. O'Kelly (President), A. Chester Beatty and John A. Costello.*

25. *The extension to the Chester Beatty Library, opened 24 August 1957.*

*26. Opening of extension to the Chester Beatty Library by the Taoiseach,
Eamon de Valera, in the presence of the President and Mrs O'Kelly,
24 August 1957.*

that they represent only one per cent of the material in
the Library . . . The Irish people will treasure one of the
most remarkable libraries in the world.[133]

Beatty's son presented him with a Distinguished Visitors'
Book to commemorate the opening of the Library. It was
specially bound in red morocco leather and decorated with
gold shamrocks. Beatty decided that the first three signatures
should be those of Mr and Mrs O'Kelly and Mr de Valera.
They had become his personal friends but their signatures
also gave an official seal of approval to the Chester Beatty
Library. The signatures of many other distinguished visitors
were entered in the Visitors' Book over the next ten years.

The Library's importance was recognised by the Department of External Affairs and by the various foreign embassies

in Dublin. It became an obligatory part of the itinerary of distinguished visitors to the city.[134] On the occasion of each visit by a foreign dignatory, Beatty arranged a reception at the Library. Each summer he hosted a garden party in the Library grounds, to which he invited Irish political leaders, members of the diplomatic corps and of the judiciary.

Boland's successors as Secretary of the Department of External Affairs maintained a keen interest in Beatty. While he was abroad, Irish diplomats met Beatty at airports, invited him to lunch and smoothed any administrative matters which arose.[135] He was provided with an Irish diplomatic passport.[136] He continued to hold a British passport until his death but he appreciated the Irish effort to facilitate him.[137]

Special efforts were made on Beatty's behalf when he expressed his intention to visit Rome and the Vatican. He had always sent a copy of his published catalogues to Cardinal Tisserant at the Vatican Library but it was one of the few major European libraries which he had not visited. A papal blessing from Pope John XXIII[138] and a visit from the Papal Legate, Cardinal Agagianian,[139] encouraged him to make the trip to Rome. (Plate 27).

Seán T. O'Kelly heard of Beatty's intended visit and he wrote to Hugh McCann, Secretary of the Department of External Affairs: 'It is up to your men in Rome to do everything possible to make his visit a success. I am sure you agree'.[140] McCann replied that he had asked Thomas Cummins, Irish Ambassador to the Holy See, 'to pay a formal call on Sir Alfred at his hotel as soon as he arrived . . . I think you may feel assured that we shall be at pains to see that all will go smoothly in Rome for Sir Alfred and his party'.[141]

Further official interest was expressed when President de Valera (who had succeeded O'Kelly in 1959) asked Cummins to enquire if Beatty could be received in private audience by Pope Paul VI as a special favour. Cummins made the necessary arrangements with the co-operation of Mgr Nasalli Rocca.[142] The visit took place from 20 to 26 April 1964 and Beatty pronounced it a great success. (Plate 28). It had convinced him of the quality of his own Library.

He wrote to Thomas McGreevy:

27. *The visit of Cardinal Agagianian to the Chester Beatty Library, 19 June 1961.*

After seeing the Oriental collections in the Vatican Library, I am afraid I was suffering from a swollen head ... It was a most enjoyable and interesting trip and we were given every facility to study the Library. I met the Pope twice, which was a very great honour, and I was most impressed by him.[143]

28. Visit to the Vatican — April 1964.
L. to R.: A. Chester Beatty, Thomas Cummins (Irish Ambassador
to the Holy See) and Pope Paul VI.

The treatment which Beatty was accorded in Rome declared him to be Ireland's foremost cultural ambassador. He enjoyed the role as much as he deserved it. The reason why he was allowed to assume it so readily depended on more than his many gifts to the Irish nation. He also had a very agreeable personality.

Portrait of a Gentleman

Chester Beatty was a much-loved figure in Dublin. He had great personal warmth and charm. Typical newspaper headlines to feature articles about him were 'Portrait of a Gentleman'[144] and 'Our Friend Sir Chester — Copper King with a Heart of Gold'.[145] Beatty was a master of public relations. One detects a certain showmanship in his adoption of Guinness: 'I always have a glass at night going to bed, or even a glass and a half, like the advertisement says!'[146] He was happy to keep a

99

keg of Guinness at his villa in the South of France. He offered a glass of champagne to a visiting British journalist but declined to join him because: 'Of course, as an honorary citizen of Ireland, I normally drink stout'.[147]

Beatty's personality was uncomplicated.[148] While he had his vanities, he had retained an appreciation of people despite his wealth. Generosity of character was his strongest asset and this seemed to grow with his advancing years. Ireland came to know an old man with a smiling face which broke easily into a hearty chuckle. He always wore a coat hung over his shoulders like a cape. (Plate 29). Claiming to have had pneumonia eight times, he was most attentive to the temperature in every room he entered. The staff and visitors at 10 Ailesbury Road often found the temperature too high as Beatty kept the heating at 70° throughout the summer.

Beatty was not a hypochondriac but he had every reason to take care of his health. He joked about his silicosis, saying that he had the most valuable pair of lungs in the world because they were full of gold dust. If someone had a cold, he would not wish to see them. He was also averse to anyone smoking in his presence and he did not allow flowers in the rooms of his house. These were some of his foibles.

The dramatic changes in society between the 1890s and the 1960s must have been a source of wonder to Beatty. He was impressed by technological advances but had no inclination to study them in his old age. He never learned to drive and preferred the comfort of a chauffeur. His staff were attentive to his every need.[149] He was very generous to them but he was a demanding employer. He would not tolerate inefficiency and his staff made certain to do as he wished. There is no doubt that he lived a pampered life style.

He was thoughtful to his friends, as men like Seán T. O'Kelly quickly learned. Beatty met the President on official occasions and found him to be a cultured man with a strong interest in books. They also met for lunch at Áras an Uachtaráin or on Saturday afternoons in County Wicklow where they each owned a house.

In 1957, President O'Kelly's Wicklow residence, Roundwood House, was destroyed by fire.[150] Beatty was upset when he heard the news and learned that the President's library had

29. Sir Chester Beatty — the smiling Grand Old Gentleman and benevolent millionaire.

101

been destroyed. He decided to form a replacement library which he would give to the President as a surprise. He arranged the purchase of 800 books of Irish interest and 400 books of general interest.[151] He acquired four oak book-cases and commissioned the Genealogical Office to design a suitable book-plate. With Mrs O'Kelly's co-operation, the library was presented to her husband on his birthday.[152]

Generous thoughts like this one endeared Beatty to Irish political leaders. He was unpretentious and valued personal friendships. He operated on the level of society in Ireland to which he had become accustomed elsewhere. He had known kings and presidents, prime ministers and industrialists, scholars and celebrities. He saw the world as his oyster and complained of 'the excess of Nationalism'.[153] President O'Kelly was correct in describing Beatty as 'a citizen of the world'. He saw no inconsistency in being American, British and Irish. In 1950 he said: 'I love Ireland and the Irish people'.[154] A year later, he wrote to General Eisenhower: 'There is one thing: there are no mining engineers in the world like the Americans'.[155] As late as 1961, he was reported as having said: 'I love Britain and I'm British now'.[156]

While Beatty had genuine feelings for Great Britain and the United States of America, Ireland held one strong advantage. The country was small, and in consequence Beatty's presence had a greater impact.

He liked to dream up schemes. Government Ministers became accustomed to receiving telephone calls from Beatty who would wish to discuss his latest plan.

In 1955 Beatty telephoned the Minister for Finance, Gerald Sweetman, and the Attorney General, Patrick McGilligan, 'to suggest ways in which the taxation of individuals in the Irish Republic could be modified so as to encourage selective immigration'.[157] He asked Selection Trust's tax adviser to compile a report on the matter and sent a copy to McGilligan. He explained the reason for his concern about the tax situation: 'Some people that I know are leaving Ireland, and they were well off, and I don't like to see them do that as I think the more people of that class here the better.'[158]

The tax consultant's report elaborated:

One of the main economic problems of the Irish Republic has been the under-development of its resources, and this under-development has largely been due to under-investment in Irish resources. To remedy this it appears necessary to secure a higher rate of investment for development purposes in Ireland, and one important step towards this would be to induce people to come into the country.

Such immigrants would inevitably pay considerable attention to the tax system and tax rates in Ireland and, of course, to the death duties, before taking up domicile there. In fact, tax inducements are likely to be the largest single factor influencing their decision.[159]

Although the Irish rates of tax and estate duty were lower than those in Great Britain, they were 'no longer of themselves likely to promote emigration'.

The differentials between the Irish and British rates of tax had fallen since Beatty's decision to move to Ireland in 1949. There was now only a shilling difference between the standard rate of income tax and 2s. 6d. between the maximum rates of tax.[160] While Beatty had no wish to suggest appropriate rates of tax, his consultant compiled a series of tables setting out the tax position in British Commonwealth countries to which wealthy Britons were retiring — South Africa, Northern and Southern Rhodesia, Tanganyika, Jersey and Guernsey.[161] Beatty felt that many of these people would be attracted to retire in Ireland if the tax rates were more favourable.

It is difficult to know the extent to which Beatty's ideas influenced Irish Government policy but he was enthusiastic when the First Programme for Economic Expansion was unveiled at the Fianna Fáil ard-fheis in 1958. He gave the Taoiseach, Seán Lemass, his support:

I have a great belief in the future of Ireland. How long has the Irish Republic been in existence? When you consider the short time and the difficulties encountered, the progress has been excellent . . . Ireland is one of the few countries in the world which will support twice its present population. Mr Lemass is doing a wonderful job in developing industries. With more capital, the future will be bright.[162]

Understandably, Beatty was interested in mineral exploration in Ireland. He was not very hopeful of finding anything:

In a country like Ireland or England where there are lush pastures and beautiful trees and the scenery is very comfortable and pleasant, you won't find very much under that. It's different where it's bare and rocky. Take a horrible place like the Klondike, well, you'll get gold. And in the frightful Congo you'll find diamonds. And think of the Arabian Gulf and those god-forsaken deserts full of oil.[163]

Nevertheless, Beatty asked his son to assist the Minister for Finance by providing documentation on mining incentives in other countries.[164] Mr Sweetman later told Dáil Éireann:

That unique opportunity of getting such an assessment of the position in every other country, even in countries in which we had no diplomatic representatives, was of very great value to us and helped considerably in developing our mining resources.[165]

Beatty had strong views about the situation at the Avoca Copper Mines in County Wicklow. He telephoned the Minister for Industry and Commerce, Jack Lynch, and arranged a meeting.[166] It was agreed that Beatty would ask Selection Trust to send over some experts to examine the mines. When the engineer's reports were received Beatty recommended the closure of the development. He was disappointed when the Irish Government ignored his advice and kept the mines open at a significant operating loss. As a tough-minded capitalist, he saw little sense in spending public money to retain jobs which would be lost, sooner or later, because of the uneconomic nature of the venture.

There is no doubt that Beatty was sincere in his assertion that Ireland had a promising future. He hoped that some of his own family would settle in the country. It delighted him when his granddaughter Anne visited Dublin during the Horse

Show week in 1955. He had everything organised so that she would have a favourable impression of the city. She had meals in the best restaurants and was taken to the theatre, the races, and a garden party was held in her honour at the Chester Beatty Library.[167] Needless to say, Anne found Dublin to be a very agreeable city and the following year she returned with her mother. Once again, Beatty arranged an itinerary including a dinner dance in a specially erected marquee in the grounds of his Library. There were many willing suitors for the hand of Beatty's granddaughter and he was thrilled when later in 1956 she announced her engagement to a Dublin man. In a fit of enthusiasm, Beatty decided to buy them a country estate as a wedding present. He purchased Clonmannon House, a fine eighteenth-century building on 600 acres, situated near Ashford in County Wicklow.[168] (Plate 30).

30. Clonmannon House, Ashford, County Wicklow.

It was most embarrassing for Beatty when the engagement fell through. He was anxious not to upset his granddaughter, so he decided that he would announce that he had bought Clonmannon for himself. The newspapers duly declared: 'Copper King Sir Alfred turns Farmer — at 84'.[169]

Beatty had kept a Guernsey herd at Calehill Park in Kent and owned 10,000 acres in Kenya devoted to cattle and maize. Clonmannon was not ideal land for farming but Beatty adopted his usual zestful approach. He made enquiries about the principal blood-lines of Aberdeen-Angus cattle and was surprised to find that a top-class bull would cost him £2,500.[170] He also contacted the Department of Lands to see how best the land could be drained. He was unimpressed by the projected cost — £4,000.[171] He decided that he would use Clonmannon as a weekend retreat and abandoned the idea of large-scale farming. A swimming pool was constructed with a glass roof to heat the water, which was pumped from the sea. Beatty enjoyed sitting at the edge, his coat draped over his shoulders, while his staff swam in the pool.[172]

Beatty was spontaneous by nature. He took decisions and formed impressions quickly. He responded generously to requests for money. His favoured Irish charitable organisation was the Wireless for the Blind Fund and for many years he was their foremost benefactor.[173] He became interested in the work of the National Council for the Blind after meeting the remarkable deaf and blind man Dr James Hanlon. The Patron of the organisation was Eamon de Valera and he encouraged Beatty to assume the role of Vice President. On two occasions, Beatty made an appeal on Radio Éireann on the organisation's behalf.[174]

While it could be said that Beatty was seeking attention by publicly making gifts to the Irish nation, his many private acts of generosity prove his sincerity. A typical instance occurred in 1961 when, aged 86, Beatty had a prostate gland operation. His staff, friends and family were very worried, his son and daughter-in-law flying to Dublin to be with him at the Meath Hospital. Beatty recovered quickly and wrote to Thomas McGreevy:

Well, I am glad to be here with you all again — it seems

it was a pretty near thing at one time — and I have made a most remarkable recovery from the operation . . . Once I have thrown off this rheumatism I feel I shall be even better than before the operation.[175]

Beatty was so delighted with the treatment which he had received at the Meath Hospital that he paid for a new heating system in the radiology unit.[176]

For a summer visitor, Beatty's contribution to the country of his adoption was quite remarkable. The extent of his munificence and his pleasant personality endeared him to Irish politicians, civil servants, journalists and the general public. The politicians chose well to treat Beatty with special consideration. The civil servants were correct in thinking him 'a person worth encouraging'.

Both politicians and civil servants hoped that Beatty would fulfil his greatest promise by bequeathing his Library to the country when he died. Their efforts to ensure that this hope would become a reality allow a unique opportunity to examine in detail a case of enlightened Irish cultural politics.

Chapter 5

Culture and Politics:
The Chester Beatty Library Bequest

A flower in the Government's button-hole.

R.J. Hayes

A Permanent Home

Chester Beatty was not the type of man to die intestate. He wished to have his affairs neatly arranged to his satisfaction. This was especially true of his art collections. He wrote: 'The problem when one is collecting a fine library is to decide as to how to dispose of it so it is of permanent benefit to future generations'.[1]

Although Beatty came to Dublin with the intention of making the city 'a permanent home' for his library, he did not have a clear idea of how he was going to guarantee its future. He had told Frederick Boland that he intended to build a private museum which he would endow in order to ensure its continuance after his death.[2] After the opening of the Chester Beatty Library in August 1953, its founder began to consider the matter in earnest.

Beatty asked Wilkinson to supply him with the address of the Pierpont Morgan Library in New York.[3] He wished to study the formula which Morgan had used to establish his library. He was impressed by the documents sent to him by the Trustees of the Morgan Library. They would form the basis on which Beatty would establish his memorial.[4]

The stated function of the Morgan Library was 'to dis-

108

seminate and contribute to the advancement of useful information and knowledge, to encourage and develop study and research and generally to conduct an institution of educational value to the public'.[5] In 1924 J.P. Morgan transferred ownership of the Library to a Board of six Trustees, together with a substantial endowment 'to secure the necessary maintenance and protection of the property'.[6]

Influenced by the Morgan Library documents, Beatty opened his Library to the public. In May 1956 he declared his intentions for its future: 'It will remain in Ireland intact. I have built this permanent home for it — though I have still to work out how I shall endow it'.[7]

Beatty did not understand the implication of this statement. He never fully realised that once he had committed himself to donating his Library to Ireland it had then ceased to be his private hobby and had become a prized national asset. His confusion on the issue is obvious from two letters which he wrote on 5 May 1956. In the first letter, Beatty refused to allow scholars to have microfilm of material from his Library before it had appeared in his published catalogues. He wrote: 'This is not a public library'.[8] Later the same day he told Wilkinson that customs duty should not be charged on purchases because:

> The Library is a semi-public library . . . it seems rather absurd that we should have to pay duty on something which will probably eventually be to the benefit of Ireland, and anyway it is to the benefit of the people of Ireland.[9]

Beatty had not yet decided whether to establish an independent foundation or to seek Irish Government sponsorship for his Library after his death. In 1957 he was forced to make up his mind. James Wilkinson died on 28 January after ten busy years as Beatty's librarian.[10] The need to choose a successor encouraged Beatty to make a definite commitment to Ireland.

The man he chose was Dr R.J. Hayes, Director of the National Library. He was well-known to Beatty and as fellow-members of the Arts Council they had developed a warm regard for each other. Hayes's career was one of brilliant achievements as scholar, linguist, librarian, bibliographer and cipher-breaker (for the Irish Intelligence Service during the Second World War).[11] A small dynamic man with a mischievous sense of humour,[12] Hayes, more than anyone else, was responsible for the eventual terms of the Chester Beatty Library bequest. He developed a formula which ensured considerable independence for the Library and also guaranteed Government sponsorship.

It was politic of Beatty to choose an influential Irishman like Hayes. He had decided that he needed a man familiar with Irish bureaucracy more than he needed an Oriental scholar. Wilkinson had been invaluable for his contacts in the museum and library world in Great Britain. Hayes was to be invaluable for his contacts in government and administration in Ireland.

Beatty asked Hayes to become Honorary Librarian. With this title Hayes felt that he could remain as Director of the National Library. Beatty was confident: 'I feel sure that the Government will make no difficulties, so I think that we can go ahead on the basis that everything is all right'.[13] Hayes advised that it would be better to seek the Government's permission before he could assume another position.

In late April, Beatty wrote to the Taoiseach, Mr de Valera:

> I do not know if I ever told you about my idea for my Library in Shrewsbury Road. I want to arrange to give this to a series of Trustees who shall hold the Library for the benefit of Ireland. I have been in touch with the Pierpont Morgan Library in New York and they have kindly sent me all the documents in reference to the organisation of that Library, and my idea is to leave my Library on more or less similar lines to those of the Morgan Library, so that Ireland will have the benefit of it.[14]

Beatty explained that he wished to offer Dr Hayes the position as his librarian because he was 'a very able man':

> This would not interfere with his duties in connection with the National Library; I simply want someone with whom I can occasionally discuss the policy, and I also want to work in my Library closely with the National

Library, so that after my death it will be organised and can run smoothly . . . I do not want to bring a librarian from England. I want to build up an Irish organisation.[15]

Beatty was optimistic to think that Hayes's involvement would not interfere with his duties at the National Library. Hayes had already moved into the Librarian's house at 20 Shrewsbury Road and he was to become heavily involved in the affairs of the Chester Beatty Library. The Taoiseach was not worried, however. De Valera replied:

I am delighted beyond measure that you propose to leave your wonderful Library for the benefit of Ireland. You may be assured that everything that I can do to meet your wishes will be done. The fact, however, is that the scheme looks so perfect that I can see no difficulties from the National Library or the Government side, and so nothing for me to do.[16]

It was not surprising that Beatty should describe de Valera as 'very co-operative . . . a very far-sighted and able man'.[17] Hayes took advantage of the amicable atmosphere to invite the Taoiseach to open the extension to the Chester Beatty Library on 24 August, 1957.[18]

Maurice Moynihan prepared the Taoiseach's speech. De Valera told him to make it short and to refer 'to the people's appreciation of Sir Chester Beatty's priceless gift to the country'.[19] While preparing the speech, Moynihan received a letter from Hayes. Beatty did not intend to mention 'anything about the Library being eventually handed over to the Irish people'. He considered this to be 'very confidential'.[20] Hayes was diplomatically suggesting that the Taoiseach should not mention anything about the future of the Chester Beatty Library. Hayes's advice was not taken too literally. In his speech de Valera said that Beatty's greatest service was to make Dublin the home of his rare and wonderful collection.[21] From a political standpoint de Valera must have been anxious to reap the positive publicity associated with Beatty, but also to remind him that in return for the Government's generous attitude it was expected that he should fulfil his promise regarding the future of the Library.

In November 1957 Hayes assumed control of the affairs of the Chester Beatty Library following the death of Wilfred Merton.[22] It was a cruel blow for Beatty to lose Wilkinson and Merton in the same year. As a result, Beatty came to rely on Hayes, who was a very different man to the two quiet Englishmen. Hayes was a strong character, formidable and, from Beatty's point of view, agreeably iconoclastic at times.[23] He competently assumed responsibility for the publishing business which had been handled by Merton. It was arranged that Hodges Figgis & Co. of Dublin would publish Beatty's catalogues in future.[24]

Beatty began to develop his ideas regarding co-operation between his own Library and the National Library. Hayes was enthusiastic and hoped that Beatty would persuade the Irish Government to build a new National Library. Beatty envisaged a large building with exhibition rooms where the public could study material of Irish interest from the National Library, Western manuscripts from Trinity College, and Oriental manuscripts from the Chester Beatty Library.[25] Beatty wrote excitedly:

> We can keep changing the exhibitions every six or nine months and we will have more space for exhibiting books and manuscripts than they will have in the British Museum . . . so for current book exhibitions Dublin will be able to compete with the great libraries of the world and the great cities of the world.[26]

Now that de Valera had made his position clear, Beatty decided to give legal weight to his pledge that he would leave his Library to Trustees for the benefit of the people of Ireland. He began to arrange the details of his Will.

A Gift to the Irish Nation

Beatty had a series of meetings with Hayes and with his solicitor Dermot McGillicuddy. By December 1958 he had formed the basis of a plan to guarantee the future of his Library. He proposed to form a Board of Trustees with Hayes as Chairman:

> I should like it to be practically a gift to the Irish

Nation but it is to remain in Dublin as long as they are sufficiently interested to keep it in good condition. I shall indicate that if they do not do this I shall leave it to some other institution, just as Pepys did in his will . . . it will compliment Trinity and Dublin will put up a very, very good show.[27]

On 2 February 1959 Beatty signed a draft codicil to his Will. He left his Library premises and contents, and the Librarian's house and its contents, to the following Trustees: Alfred Chester Beatty Junior, Dermot McGillicuddy, James Cecil Hosking, Sheila Viscountess Powerscourt, Thomas A. McGreevy, George A. Duncan, Dr Richard J. Hayes, and the Director for the time being of the National Library.

Beatty charged the Trustees with the task 'to keep and maintain my said Library for the use and enjoyment of the public'. He directed that 'without imposing any obligation on them', the Trustees 'shall have regard to the Charter Constitution and By-Laws and other basic documents of the Pierpont Morgan Library to see in what manner they can be utilised and adapted for the general benefit and preservation of my Library'.

The Trustees were not permitted to sell any of the contents other than minor furnishings. If the conditions of the Will were infringed, Beatty (using Pepys's method) bequeathed the premises and contents to the library of Princeton University in New Jersey.[28] He left £40,000 to the Trustees to use for the maintenance and preservation of the Library (including the employment of a librarian and staff). The power of appointing new Trustees was vested in the surviving Trustees and Beatty directed: 'I would like as far as possible for a member of my Family or a descendant of mine always to be a Trustee'.

Beatty sent a copy of this draft to Hayes with the request that he study the Morgan papers and sort out the matter. He was apologetic about giving Hayes more work but did so 'because I want you to be Chairman of the Committee when I go, and it is very important that you have it in a form where you can handle the business with a minimum amount of worry'.[29] After studying the proposed formula, Hayes replied:

'It seems to me perfectly adapted for the purpose it is to serve. Every power given to the Pierpont Morgan Trustees is included and moreover, included in a less rigid form, which is all the better'.[30] Hayes suggested a number of minor verbal changes and a rearrangement of the paragraphs to make the document more logical. He proposed that Group Captain Charles Tighe (Beatty's farm manager at Clonmannon Estate) should be included as a Trustee. He thought that the Trustees should have power to receive gifts of funds or of books, manuscripts and objects; that they should be permitted to buy additional material if funds were sufficient; and that they should be empowered to allow items on loan from the collections. If the Trust failed, Hayes considered that Princeton should also receive any catalogues and publications then in stock. Hayes noted: 'Why keep the harness if you part with the horse?'[31]

This last comment was typical of Hayes and it recalls another phrase which has been wrongly attributed to Beatty. It is said that Beatty did not leave a large endowment fund because he remarked: 'If you give a man a racehorse you don't give him oats to feed it as well'.[32] Hayes liked to use this phrase to justify Beatty's actions. The matter is a complicated one and there are a number of possible explanations. It could be argued that Hayes was justifying his own actions in encouraging Beatty that the Irish Government should assume responsibility for the Chester Beatty Library. Further, Hayes and others in Beatty's circle stood to gain more from Beatty's will if he did not endow his Library. A second view suggests that Beatty's primary concern was to provide for his family and friends. Once this had been done, he found that he had not enough money left to endow his Library.

Essentially the argument depends on whether Beatty or Hayes controlled policy. The evidence indicates that Beatty provided the general guidelines and Hayes took care of the details. Beatty accepted all of Hayes's comments on his draft Will. While Beatty's family and friends may have attempted to exert influence on him, it is clear that his primary concern was indeed to provide for them. Beatty owned considerable property but his financial resources were being depleted. He wrote to McGreevy: 'I have been living on capital for the last fifteen years and reduced my estate very, very materially'.[33]

114

The payment of death duties on his wife's estate was an additional drain on Beatty's resources. He complained: 'The death duties come to a very large sum and I have not got the cash available to pay for them without selling some of the things'.[34]

It was an expensive process establishing a library in Dublin. Beatty's expenses included the cost of buildings,[35] the purchase of his art collections,[36] the publications business, conservation, the visits of scholars, staff salaries, and maintenance of the Library.[37] Beatty's financial contributions to charitable institutions must also be considered.[38]

These factors encouraged Beatty to negotiate a deal with the Irish Government. He could not be another Pierpont Morgan. He explained to Hayes: 'I can only leave a moderate endowment which will probably pay the taxes and perhaps a very few employees'.[39] He limited his plans by emphasising: 'I think the Library will always have to be an exhibition library'.[40] He was delighted with Hayes's efforts to publicise the contents. A booklet written by Hayes proclaimed the treasures of 'the greatest collection of Oriental manuscripts ever made by a private collector'.[41] (Plate 31). Beatty advised: 'It is a good idea to send a copy of the brochure to de Valera, Costello and, of course, the President'.[42]

Beatty felt that he could not provide a reading room for scholars. He wrote: 'It would be quite expensive . . . as one not only has to have a room but also someone to supervise it. It seems to me that will eventually be handled through the National Library'.[43] This opinion was reinforced in March 1959 when Beatty received a letter from W.E.D. Allen, a widely-travelled man who had settled in County Waterford.[44] Allen had been revising his Will and he wondered if Beatty would be prepared to accept his library of books on Turkey, Russia and Caucasia. It could be housed at the Chester Beatty Library in a room marked 'Allen Bequest'. Allen presumed that Beatty's Library would not be subject to death duties. He hoped that by presenting his library to Beatty he could also avoid the duties.

Beatty appreciated Allen's predicament but he could not see how he could accommodate another library. He wrote to Hayes that the ideal place for Allen's library would be in a

31. Indian Miniature — Dancing Girls — Mughal School, eighteenth century (courtesy of Trustees of the CBL).

new National Library.[45] It should be noted that Beatty's comment reflected media speculation that the Government was looking for a site for a new National Library. Hayes kept Beatty briefed on the matter. They both realised that it would relieve pressure on the Chester Beatty Library. Beatty argued:

> We have no facilities whatsoever, and I do not see how we are going to have for this reason: It means a large organisation and the Government of Ireland may not wish to supply the Chester Beatty Library with that organisation, because we have not as a rule so many books to study, outside of the Arabic.[46]

Beatty wrote to Allen thanking him for his generous offer but telling him of his inability to accept it.[47] Beatty felt sure that Allen's library would not attract death duties if Allen prepared matters by making his intentions known to the Irish Government.

Beatty was unaware that there had recently been an embarrassing situation within the Irish civil service. It concerned the letter to de Valera in which Beatty's hopes for the Chester Beatty Library had first been declared to the Government. The affair began when Maurice Moynihan found a rough note of a conversation he had with Tarlach Ó Raifeartaigh, Secretary of the Department of Education, on 25 May 1957.[48] The note indicated that Chester Beatty had offered his art collection to the nation and that de Valera had written to thank him. Moynihan realised the importance of this correspondence and wished to trace the letters. The Department of Education was unable to find them. Moynihan's Assistant Secretary, Dr Nolan, searched the Taoiseach's office but it was to no avail. When President de Valera was asked about the matter he confused the issue by expressing doubt that the correspondence had ever taken place. Nolan wrote to Moynihan: 'Mr Ó Raifeartaigh's discussions with you seem to indicate quite clearly, however, that there was, in fact, such correspondence'.[49]

Nolan contacted Hayes and asked him if, without alerting Beatty, he could confirm the existence of the correspondence. Hayes obliged by forwarding a copy of de Valera's letter of 6 May 1957. Beatty's letter finally turned up in October 1960 during a tidying up of miscellaneous papers in the

117

Department of Education.[50] President de Valera was very relieved to hear of the discovery.[51] Presumably he ordered that Beatty's correspondence should be treated less casually in future.

Beatty's faith in the workings of Irish bureaucracy would have been dented if he had heard of this embarrassing affair, but the matter remained within the civil service. Instead, Beatty initiated the next stage in the negotiations regarding his Library bequest.

The Fine Art of Cultural Politics

W.E.D. Allen's opinion that the Chester Beatty Library would not be subject to death duties encouraged Beatty to make certain that this would be the case. He asked Hayes to seek the legal position from Dermot McGillicuddy.[52] Hayes learned that the Chester Beatty Library would not be subject to estate duty because it was considered to be of national importance. Nevertheless, estate duty would be charged on the endowment fund, on the buildings and furnishings, and on the publications available for sale. Hayes estimated that the total amount liable for duty would be about £80,000. He wrote:

> It seems outrageous to have to pay duty on this very large sum when one is giving as a free gift something worth over £2 million. It must be remembered, however, that all gifts for "charitable purposes" in Ireland are liable for estate duty, and that if anyone left £100,000 to a Dublin hospital or a university, estate duty would be paid. To treat the Chester Beatty Library differently would therefore create a precedent, but I believe that the Government has sufficient appreciation of the munificence of Sir Chester's bequest to be prepared to make an exception in his case.[53]

Hayes suggested three possible ways of having the duty remitted in a manner which would be satisfactory to Beatty and to the Government. The first method was to form a company with Beatty as Chairman and a shadow board which would obey his wishes in every respect. The second possibility was to ask the Government to pass an Act remitting in advance the duty on the Beatty bequest because of its unprecedented value and interest to the nation.

Hayes thought that the first possibility would not appeal to Beatty and the second would not be of interest to the Government. He thought the third possibility to be the best solution. Beatty would ask the Government to make a binding agreement to accept the Chester Beatty Library on his death as a gift to the nation. He would offer this gift on certain conditions: (i) that the Government would pay or remit any estate duty involved; (ii) that the Government would give an annual grant-in-aid sufficient to maintain the Library as a learned library, kept as a unit apart from all other institutions and open to those competent to use it; (iii) that the administration of the Library, including the selection of and the appointment of the staff, would be vested in a self-perpetuating Board of Trustees exactly as set out in the form of bequest already drawn up. If the Government asked to have the right to nominate additional Trustees, it should be insisted that they must not exceed one-third of the total number.[54]

Hayes was familiar with the similar arrangements at the National Library. It was founded through the efforts of the Royal Dublin Society and a system had been preserved whereby eight of the Trustees were elected by the R.D.S. and four by the Government. The Dublin Institute for Advanced Studies was an example of an institution dependent on government funds but having complete autonomy in the direction of its affairs.

It is important to state that it was Hayes who proposed the scheme which was eventually to form the basis of the organisation of the Chester Beatty Library after the death of its founder. Beatty had set out the guidelines in the draft codicil to his Will. He had told Hayes to shape the details in the form which would cause the least worry.

Hayes advised Beatty that the favoured proposal outlined to McGillicuddy had a number of advantages. The Board of Trustees would be independent but no endowment fund would be necessary. The alternative was to make the Trustees financially independent, but Beatty was unable to leave an adequate endowment fund. Hayes argued that with the

119

changing values of money, even a large endowment might prove insufficient. Sooner or later the Trustees would have to seek a government grant-in-aid. He wrote: 'You are in a better bargaining position now than the Trustees would be in then. You can now demand perpetual maintenance plus full powers of administration for the Trustees'.[55]

With this policy in mind, Hayes telephoned Maurice Moynihan. He said that he had been requested by Beatty to seek an interview with the Taoiseach, Mr Lemass, to discuss the question of estate duty arising from Beatty's intention to leave his Library to the Nation.[56] Beatty asked Hayes to send the Taoiseach a copy of the codicil to his Will so that his intentions would be known to the Government.[57]

On 6 December 1960, Hayes and McGillicuddy met Lemass at Leinster House. After the meeting Lemass wrote: 'I undertook to put the question to the Minister for Finance and to urge that he should consider it sympathetically, and I told the visitors that they could inform Sir Chester that I was so doing'.[58]

Beatty was delighted to be able to leave these complicated matters to Hayes. He wrote cheerfully about his Library:

> I think it will be appreciated very much more 50 or 100 years after we are both gone than it is today. I am quite surprised that I was able to make this collection. It is far finer than I had any conception of. They say the Good Lord looks after drunken people and children. As I never drank to any extent, I must come under the children's category. You are doing a wonderful job of pulling the Library into shape, and I think as time goes on we will have more of these visitors.[59]

While Beatty was musing contentedly, the question of remitting estate duty on his Library bequest was being considered in Government circles. On Lemass's instructions Dr Nolan wrote to T.K. Whitaker, Secretary of the Department of Finance:

> The Taoiseach would be glad if, in the altogether exceptional circumstances of the case, the Minister could see his way to accede to Sir Chester Beatty's request that the buildings (including their furnishings) and the endow-

ment fund of the Chester Beatty Library be exempted from estate duty on his death.[60]

The Minister for Finance, Dr James Ryan, agreed to support the case. Whitaker contacted Seán Réamonn to advise him about the matter. While there was a precedent for such an exemption in the special Act of 1932 regarding the gift of the Bourn-Vincent Estate at Killarney, the relevant Finance Act (1931; Section 28) would cover exemption from death duty of the Chester Beatty Library only, not the property (buildings and grounds, furnishings and endowment fund). The Minister therefore asked Réamonn to consider what provision might appropriately be made in the following year's Finance Bill to cover the property as well as the Library.[61] The desired provision duly appeared in the Finance Act of 1961. Couched in legal jargon, it read:

Property the subject matter of a gift to the State taking effect in possession in the donor's lifetime or on his death shall not be included in the property passing or deemed to pass on his death where the death occurs after the passing of this Act.[62]

This subsection was qualified:

An exemption . . . shall apply so long (and only so long) as the property comprised in the gift continues under the terms of the gift to be held exclusively for the use and enjoyment or benefit of the public.[63]

The Irish Government had altered the law of the State in order to facilitate the wishes of Sir Chester Beatty. It was a personal success for Hayes and he was understandably delighted. He wrote to Beatty, deliberately exaggerating the scale of the representations made:

I am writing to thank you and congratulate you on the new Irish budget. It is quite clear from the contents that you must have drawn it up and persuaded the Government to adopt it. I see you knocked eleven per cent off the top of the Estate Duty rate — a proposal for which you had repeatedly pressed, then you brought down the

income tax to 6/4 and raised the sur tax level. As you
don't smoke you put a penny on cigarettes. You have
increased the subsidy for lime and phosphates for Clonmannon. I miss only one thing — a special tax on fisher-
men who export lobsters. A fine job all round. We are
delighted with it.[64]

If anyone deserved congratulations, it was Hayes himself and
not Beatty. But Hayes had learned, like Brendan Bracken,
that Beatty enjoyed 'lots of flattery'.[65]

One must consider to what extent Hayes was acting out of
self-interest in his relationship with Beatty. After all, he
received a house at Shrewsbury Road rent-free, and a substantial salary with an entertainment allowance. Beatty left
him six per cent of his residuary estate in his Will. It would
be easy to say that it was in Hayes's financial interest to
make sure that Beatty's wishes were obeyed. But it is also
true that Hayes and Beatty were good friends and each had
respect for the other's talents and achievements. Hayes paid
attention to detail, sending Beatty a ham at Christmas, a
salmon for his birthday. Beatty appreciated these little gestures
and came to trust Hayes more than anyone else. Hayes's real
importance lies in the time and energy which he spent in
guaranteeing that the Chester Beatty Library would remain in
Dublin for the benefit of the Irish people. In this sense, Hayes
was acting in the public interest.

Hayes also knew that his efforts were subject to a time
limit. He believed that the Government would co-operate
while Beatty was alive to act as a lever. Experience had
taught Hayes that the Government was slow to commit itself
to large expense on a cultural matter. It was with a mixture
of astonishment and enthusiasm that Hayes wrote to Beatty
in October 1961:

Now for the big news. You will see from enclosed cut-
tings that the Government has bought a site for a new
National Library. It is about half-way between Kildare
Street, where we are now, and Shrewsbury Road . . .
It was put up for auction and this forced the Department
of Education to make a quick decision — a thing which
Government departments abhor. I assume, though as

yet I have heard nothing, that they will go ahead with the planning and construction without any delay.[66]

Hayes's dream was short-lived. Following a general election, Fianna Fáil was returned to office and it became clear that the plans for a new National Library were not considered to be urgent. Hayes was disgusted. His hopes had been shattered once again and he began to turn his attention away from the National Library. He devoted more and more time to refining the details of the Chester Beatty Library bequest.

Beatty was aware that the future of his Library would have to be secured before he died. The illness which resulted in a prostate gland operation gave him a fright. When he had recovered, he arranged a meeting with his solicitor. The death of his daughter in May 1962 had further necessitated a reorganisation of his legal affairs.

Beatty arranged to dispose of his property in six different Wills — one each for Ireland, France, Portugal, Jersey, Egypt and Kenya. He bequeathed the properties in Portugal and in Egypt to his son. The property in France was left to his son, his granddaughters (Anne Newling and Lady Sarah Brooke) and his great-grandson (the Hon. Guy Brooke). The properties in Jersey and Kenya were to be sold. Beatty also established a United Kingdom Family Trust worth £1,750,000 from which his two granddaughters would benefit.

While Beatty was considering his Irish Will, McGillicuddy suggested that it would be better to include the Library bequest in the Will proper rather than in a codicil.[67] Beatty agreed that this should be done. He had decided not to increase the sum of £40,000 which he had left to maintain the Library: 'That means that the Government must keep the Library going. Of course, it will cost very little in comparison to what it means to Ireland'.[68]

Beatty had correctly gauged the mood of the Irish Government. He knew that it had been decided at official level that the Chester Beatty Library would become a national institution when he died, the subject of state sponsorship. The Government knew that Beatty did not intend to leave a substantial trust fund.

Hayes had thought it likely that if the Government agreed

to an annual grant-in-aid to the Chester Beatty Library, it would probably seek to nominate some of the Trustees. Beatty felt that 'the Government should have the right to nominate a certain number' since he was making the State pay for the Library.[69] He asked McGillicuddy to investigate the matter.

It is difficult to avoid the conclusion that once Beatty had succeeded in having the law changed to suit him regarding estate duty, he adopted a more imperious attitude towards the Irish Government. He had been made aware of his own importance and it was tempting for him to abuse it.

It must have been irritating at times for Irish Government officials to calmly read of record prices paid in London sale-rooms for art objects from Beatty's collections. While Beatty was deciding not to increase the trust fund in his Will above £40,000, his collection of watches and gold boxes was sold at Sotheby's for £124,029.[70]

One person who cannot have felt too kindly towards Beatty was James G. Coleman. He was Registrar of the Pharmaceutical Society of Ireland, which had its premises at 18 Shrewsbury Road beside the Chester Beatty Library. In October 1963, Coleman wrote to J.R. Whitty of the Department of Finance: 'You will remember that I mentioned, off the record, something which is a source of worry'.[71] Coleman explained that Beatty wanted to buy a strip of the Society's front lawn, even though they had already sold him a strip bordering their Biology Laboratory:

> He is putting pressure on us by saying that an American University would be only too glad to pay him millions of dollars for the Library he proposes leaving to the State. We are most anxious not to deprieve [sic] the country of such a valuable asset. As I mentioned to you, we believe that some influential member of the Government should be "tipped off" about this position. It is possible that influence could be brought to bear on the R.D.S. to give Sir Chester some of their land. Perhaps it would be possible for you to drop a hint in the right quarter.[72]

Whitty wrote to Tadhg Ó Cearbhaill, Assistant Secretary,

Department of the Taoiseach, to say that he had advised Coleman that 'we might be able to do something in the matter'.[73] Ó Cearbhaill ascertained that the approach to Coleman had been made by Beatty personally. On the advice of the Taoiseach, Ó Cearbhaill wrote to Professor James Meenan, Chairman of the Executive Committee of the R.D.S.:

> There appears to be some risk that, if Sir Chester Beatty is unable to obtain the land he requires, some of his collection, which he intends to leave to the nation, will be disposed of to institutions abroad. It has been suggested to the Taoiseach that the Royal Dublin Society might be in a position to sell a small portion of their land to Sir Chester Beatty in the interest of preventing a dispersal of the collection. The Taoiseach has asked me to convey to you his concern at the situation and to enquire whether the Royal Dublin Society would be open to consider an approach from Sir Chester Beatty for the land which he requires.[74]

Meenan understood the Taoiseach's anxiety and replied:

> Generally speaking, we would certainly see if there was anything we could do to facilitate Sir Chester Beatty. Perhaps it would be possible for him to get in touch with us so that we can discuss exactly what may be involved.[75]

Beatty had left Dublin to spend the winter as usual in the South of France. The matter could be left in abeyance until his return the following summer.[76] As it happened, Beatty did not pursue his attempt to acquire more land for his Library. His attention was distracted by an intriguing letter which he received from Dr Martin Bodmer.[77]

The Swiss art collector had been considering the future of his library.[78] He had not decided on a particular formula and it worried him that his life's work would not be secured in a permanent institution. He had visited Dublin for the Red Cross Convention in 1962 and Beatty had entertained him at 10 Ailesbury Road. The formula which Bodmer now suggested was certainly an imaginative one. He proposed the establishment of a Bodmer-Beatty Foundation. Bodmer thought that if the two most important private libraries in the world were joined, 'the world would be dazzled, they would cast into the shade the British Museum'. He asked Beatty:

> I wonder if a formula could be found to unite both our creations without prejudicing in the least the personal character of each one? It would be no question to touch upon the structure, the name or seat of them. They could even stay in Dublin and Geneva. I envisage only the possibility of an organised collaboration and eventually a common foundation. Do you think it is any use to pursue this idea? It seems to me that it could be something very great. What an event for scholars, librarians, connoisseurs, students and almost everybody interested in culture ... I may be wrong in your eyes but I am on the tiptoe of expectation about your opinion.[79]

Beatty considered Bodmer's suggestion for over a month before sending his reply. This letter is the best summary of Beatty's views on the role of the art collector and of his hopes for his own Library. He sympathised with Bodmer — all art collectors shared the same predicament:

> The great problem, after all the time, trouble and expense in arriving at a final result, is that the whole thing is liable to be split up into a thousand pieces and scattered over a hundred different American libraries and museums, and can never be centred as a whole. That has bothered me a great deal ... Another thing is that if one left it to one of the great libraries or museums, the result is that it would simply go down to the cellars ... I hesitate to guess as to how many fine paintings are stored in places like the National Gallery of England in London ... they might just as well have been thrown in the sea for all the benefit the public will get from them.[80]

In response to Bodmer's proposal that they should form some sort of common foundation, Beatty wrote:

> Your suggestion is an interesting one, but I am afraid it is not practicable, because I have more or less settled all the details in connection with mine. I have discussed the matter with de Valera, the President of Ireland, and Dr

Hayes, who is head of the National Library of Ireland, has worked on the matter . . . I have transferred it to a committee beginning with six and ending with twelve, and I have tried to keep it out of politics . . . I do not intend to give them an endowment. I will give them a small amount of money to run the Library until they work out all the details . . . It must remain as a unit, as it is now, and they must not dispose of any of the contents.

The Chester Beatty Library was firmly associated with Ireland. Equally, Beatty advised Bodmer: 'Yours is associated with Switzerland. Your library is there and it seems to me that in all probability you will always want it to remain in Switzerland for the benefit of the Swiss people'.[81]

It is clear that Beatty was proud that his Library would forever be associated with Dublin. He knew the importance of his friendship with de Valera, who had assured him that everything would be done to meet his wishes. In 1965, legislation was again altered at Beatty's request.

In August of the previous year, Hayes had written to Dr Nolan of the Taoiseach's Department. The letter was written in a bravura style designed to shake any bureaucratic complacency:

I think I should let you know that the Succession Bill, 1964, recently circulated has some consequences which were not foreseen. It would, if it became law in its present form, involve the sale of the Chester Beatty Library.[82]

Hayes explained that Beatty's estate other than his Library would be insufficient to meet the required legal shares of his family. The Bill might also discourage other people with large estates from settling in Ireland because it limited so severely their power of disposition of their property. Hayes suggested that a simple amendment would resolve the situation. It would read: 'Where the net value after payment of duty of a testator's estate is in excess of £100,000, the legal rights of spouse and issue shall be limited to their shares of £100,000'.

Nolan wrote to Peter Berry, Secretary of the Department of Justice: 'Perhaps you would be so good as to let me know in due course whether your Minister can see his way to do anything to meet the point which Dr Hayes raises'.[83]

When the Succession Act, 1965, was passed by the Dáil it contained a sub-section which resolved the difficulty regarding the Chester Beatty Library. Since Beatty's wife had predeceased him, the relevant part of the Act concerned the provision for children. Hayes was happy that it could not be proven that Beatty 'had failed in his moral duty to make proper provision' for his son.[84] In fact, quite the opposite was true.

Having successfully offset the danger of the Succession legislation, Beatty decided to complete the details of his Library bequest. It seemed an opportune moment as he celebrated his ninetieth birthday and received messages of congratulations from President de Valera and the Taoiseach, Seán Lemass.[85]

Beatty asked the future Trustees of the Chester Beatty Library to write to the Taoiseach on his behalf.[86] He wanted an assurance from the Government that an extension would be built to his Library if he bequeathed it to the Irish nation. Hayes knew that Beatty was testing the Government's commitment. For years a new National Library had been promised but no Government had been willing to provide the necessary finance. Would the Government be prepared to spend money on the Chester Beatty Library? Hayes realised that a strong case would have to be advanced and he carefully drafted the letter for Beatty. He began by stressing the importance of the Library:

As you are no doubt aware, the contents of the Library at present market values are worth between three and a half and four million pounds, and to place figures on it is no measure of its importance to the country as a cultural acquisition since most of the items in the collections, such as the earliest text of the Bible, are irreplaceable. It contains a representative collection of the finest manuscripts of all the civilisations western and oriental from the earliest time up to the present day. Its collections forge a link between Ireland and most of the emerging countries of Africa and Asia. As the catalogues are being distributed throughout the world, it is engaging the attention of scholars in Europe, the United States and many Eastern countries and attracting them to Ireland in increasing numbers. Its potential for the future in this respect cannot be overestimated.

While Sir Chester Beatty is glad to hand over these priceless collections as a free gift to Ireland, he is naturally anxious that the collections should be adequately displayed... The exhibition space available in the buildings now existing in the Chester Beatty Library permit the showing of a small fraction of what should be on view.

Sir Chester has accordingly requested us to seek from you an assurance that the Government would be prepared within a fixed period after his death to erect additional exhibition rooms adjacent to the present site so that the collections could be adequately displayed.

It is realised, of course, that you cannot bind future governments in a matter of this kind, but it is felt that an approval in principle of the project would reassure Sir Chester Beatty on the question of the adequate display of his treasures in perpetuity.[87]

Lemass said that he would make arrangements to bring the matter before the Government for consideration.[88] He wrote to the Minister for Finance, Jack Lynch:

I assume that you see no difficulty in giving the assurance regarding the extension of the Library as desired by Chester Beatty. I think this should be a formal Government decision. On learning that you agree, I will arrange to have the matter submitted to the Government at an early meeting.[89]

Lynch replied: 'I see no difficulty in giving the assurance provided that the Trustees will not be unreasonable about the size of the extension or the period within which it should be provided'.[90]

Tadhg Ó Cearbhaill prepared a memorandum for the Government. He noted that the Taoiseach considered the Trustees' request to be a reasonable one and that the Minister for Finance had also agreed to the proposal. In an enclosed minute, Ó Cearbhaill wrote pointedly:

> The overriding consideration now is the desirability of giving the assurance quickly lest Sir Chester Beatty, now 91 years of age, might be tempted to make any change in his Will and send some of his art treasures elsewhere, to the country's loss.[91]

This was precisely the reaction which Hayes had anticipated.

The Government authorised Lemass to write to the Trustees, giving the assurance 'that additional exhibition rooms adjacent to the present site will be provided out of public funds, within a reasonable period of years after the death of Sir Chester Beatty'.[92] The Taoiseach added: 'I should like to take this opportunity of asking you to convey to Sir Chester my best wishes for his health and personal wellbeing'.[93]

Beatty was thrilled with the Government's assurance. He asked Hayes to thank Lemass. Hayes wrote that the Taoiseach's letter had 'added immeasurably to the happiness of Sir Chester Beatty and has served to confirm his conviction that Ireland, because of its deep interest in cultural matters, was the most suitable home for his treasures'.[94]

Hayes thanked each of the Trustees for their support. He could hardly believe that they had succeeded, and wrote: 'What a wonderfully satisfactory and well-phrased reply we got! Sir Chester is beside himself with delight'.[95] Beatty was particularly grateful to the Chief Justice, Cearbhall Ó Dálaigh. Hayes wrote: 'Both he and I appreciate how much weight was added to the application by the presence of your signature'.[96]

Beatty had made his intentions clear on many occasions when speaking to journalists. But the Government's assurance prompted him to announce formally that he would leave his Library to the Irish people. He joked: 'I am very fond of the people of Ireland, and I can't take it with me. It might get burned up if I did'.[97]

Lemass followed up his letter to the Library Trustees by asking the Office of Public Works to investigate how best to extend the facilities at Shrewsbury Road.[98] A report was prepared by J.P. Alcock, Assistant Principal Architect, following a meeting with Hayes. Alcock did not agree with Hayes's proposal that an extension could be built by acquiring land from the Pharmaceutical Society. This proposal had already caused difficulty and Alcock felt that the site was unsuitable. He concluded: 'The whole question of extending the institution and particularly site problems is surrounded by serious difficulties'.[99]

Raymond McGrath, Chief Architect of the O.P.W., suggested that, since the site at Shrewsbury Road was unsuitable for extension, it might be better to look for entirely new premises. The O.P.W. resurrected the proposals for a new National Library and told Hayes that the Chester Beatty Library could be catered for on the site which had been acquired in 1961. Understandably, Hayes was not impressed. He politely replied that the Taoiseach had agreed to an extension at Shrewsbury Road.[100]

Hayes was in total control at the Chester Beatty Library. Beatty was becoming feeble with age and had stopped collecting. He considered that his work was done. He asked Hayes and Alexis Fitzgerald (who had replaced McGillicuddy as his solicitor) to draw up a revised version of his Irish Will. The summer of 1966 was spent quietly in Dublin. It was known that Beatty had not been well in the spring. On 17 August he was pleased to receive President and Mrs de Valera when they paid a visit to his Library.[101] They were to be the last visitors to see Beatty at 20 Shrewsbury Road. (Plate 32). On 19 August he signed his revised Will bequeathing the Library to a Board of Trustees for the benefit of the public. Two days later he left for the South of France.

There were many changes in the Will compared to that drawn up in 1959. Most of the alterations were the work of Hayes. He had taken Beatty's general ideas and refined them into a very precise document. It is no exaggeration to say that Beatty trusted Hayes enough to allow him to write the section of his Will regarding his Library. The executors of the revised Will were James Hosking, John Wooderson, Group Captain Tighe and Raymond O'Neill (Senior Counsel and brother of Joan O'Neill). The named Trustees of the Chester Beatty Library were Dr R.J. Hayes, Terence de Vere White, Cearbhall Ó Dálaigh, Dr C.S. Andrews and James Hosking. Beatty's family would not be involved with the Library after his death. His son declined an invitation to become a Trustee.

All reference to the Pierpont Morgan Library was removed, though the Morgan formula still formed the basis of the Beatty bequest. The amount left to maintain the Library between the date of Beatty's death and the handing over to the Trustees was reduced to £10,000. Beatty requested that one of his Trustees (of whom there was to be a maximum of 12) should be appointed by the President of Ireland and another by the Taoiseach. Hayes had reluctantly agreed that this provision was desirable because 'In dealing with the Government for funds the Trustees would be in a better bargaining situation if they were in a position to offer one or two trusteeships to Government nominees'.[102] Hayes had been worried about having Government nominees on the Board:

32. The last visitors to see Chester Beatty at his Library, Mr and Mrs de Valera, 17 August 1966.

They would be there as a matter of right and might be tempted to exercise undue control in return for damn little. There is also the danger that the Government would be tempted to offer the trusteeships to please political supporters or appease political opponents, or reward useless types. They might nominate some Gaelic enthusiast who would want all the notices put up in Irish as well as English.[103]

Hayes thought it best to name as few Trustees as possible:

It will be regarded as a high honour to be a Trustee of the Chester Beatty Library and it could well be very useful in the years ahead to be able to offer a Trusteeship to a very wealthy man who would help the Library financially or perhaps hand over a valuable collection of some kind.[104]

Hayes's cynicism about Irish attitudes reached its peak in his advocacy of a safeguard clause in Beatty's Will. He advised 'that the proviso regarding Princeton should go. It is certainly unnecessary and seems like a vote of no confidence in the appreciation by the people or government of the gift'.[105] Nevertheless, Hayes argued:

If the Princeton provision is removed it would seem necessary to include in this section a similar power of sale in the most unlikely event of no government or other funds becoming available for the maintenance of the collection as a public institution. This power would, of course, only be used in the most dire circumstances and only after appeals to the Government and general public had failed, but it seems necessary nonetheless to include it in order to meet every possible eventuality.[106]

Hayes suggested a failsafe scheme, which Beatty adopted. If the Irish Government had not provided funds to build an extension within six years of Beatty's death, the Trustees were empowered to sell the biblical papyri. This was ingenious. Hayes knew that the Irish people would never permit the Government to sell the papyri, which were renowned as among the earliest evidence of Christianity.[107]

On Hayes's recommendation, the use of the Chester Beatty Library was not to be limited to the 'Public of Ireland'. It would be 'for the use of the Public' whether Irish or from other countries.[108] Hayes thought that the Director of the National Library should be a Trustee but 'should not necessarily be Chairman in my absence. I am made Chairman not because I am Director of the National Library but because I know your wishes better than any other Trustee and also because I know the collections better than anyone else'.[109]

Without imposing any legal obligation, Beatty's Will declared the desire that one or more Trustees should be appointed from among lecturers or professors of Oriental Languages in Dublin University, the National University of Ireland or Queen's University, Belfast.[110] The quorum for meetings of the Library Trustees was to be five. In the event of an equality of votes on a decision, the Chairman, chosen from among the Trustees and by them, would have a second casting vote.[111]

Beatty did not leave any of his residuary estate to the Library Trustees. It was to be divided into ten parts, one tenth to be used for charitable purposes, the other nine tenths to be distributed in specified proportions to 17 named people.[112] The Trustees would have to secure an annual grant-in-aid from the Government. By leaving no endowment, Beatty forced the Government to sponsor the Library as a national institution. He did, however, offer a financial incentive. He directed that after the termination of the periods stated in two Trust Funds which he had established (one on 28 October 1959 and the other on 15 May 1961), the amounts therein should be transferred to the Trustees of the Chester Beatty Library.[113]

During the negotiations with the Government, Beatty had used many of the tactics which he had learned in the world of mining finance. He had shown a mixture of self-interest and philanthropy. The Government was content that the prize of the Chester Beatty Library had been secured for Ireland. They never considered that Beatty might change his mind before he died.

A Secret Crisis

Once Beatty had signed the revised version of his Irish Will, Hayes felt free to pursue his own interests. He was supervising a bibliography of documents of Irish interest which were stored in libraries and archives throughout the world. He was a compulsive worker and became preoccupied with this awesome task. He tried to reduce his paper-work at the Chester Beatty Library to a minimum so that he could work undisturbed in the Librarian's house.

Hayes held the view that the Library was of limited appeal since it was so specialised. It would be some time before the Irish people would come in substantial numbers. They would have to be educated to appreciate the treasures which Beatty had entrusted to them. In the meantime, the Library was just 'a flower in the Government's button-hole'.[114] Hayes wrote to Beatty:

> Visitors to a library of this kind will always tend to be confined to those with a high appreciation of art, or with a knowledge of the oriental world, to connoisseurs and scholars, to highly cultured people rather than the masses.[115]

Hayes should have known that this type of comment was unlikely to please Beatty. The Library was pledged to a country which did not have many scholars or connoisseurs who specialised in Oriental art. By stressing this fact, Hayes worried Beatty. The elderly benefactor began to consider ways to ensure a wider audience.

For many years Beatty had maintained contact with the authorities of Princeton University and Columbia University. They courted him and he supported them financially.[116] He had particularly fond memories of Princeton University Library and was curious to know how his own Library compared with it. Robert Garrett, a classmate of Beatty's at Princeton, had presented a collection of rare Oriental manuscripts to the University in 1942. The Princeton Librarian, William S. Dix, visited the Chester Beatty Library in 1964 and Beatty heard a description of the Garrett collection.

Hayes had encouraged Beatty to drop the clause in his Will

which bequeathed the Chester Beatty Library to Princeton University if the Irish Government failed to fulfil their promise regarding an extension. Perhaps this inspired Beatty to help Princeton in another way. In July 1966 he wrote to the President of Princeton University, Dr Robert F. Goheen, expressing the hope 'that a way could be found to offer the large number of Western and Oriental manuscripts and miniatures which I have found to scholars in the United States'.[117] The Princeton authorities were delighted and they could be forgiven for thinking that Beatty intended to leave his art collections, or at least part of them, to their University. It was decided that Beatty would send a selection of his manuscripts to Princeton for an exhibition which would open in February 1967. This exhibition would be the first of a series of exhibitions of material from the Chester Beatty Library.

A month after writing to Dr Goheen, Beatty signed his Will and left for the South of France. He had added a codicil to the Will withdrawing from inclusion in the gift of his Library, 27 named manuscripts.[118] The reason for this decision is unclear. Perhaps Beatty felt that his Library was primarily an Oriental one and it was therefore appropriate to send his Western manuscripts for sale where they would probably be bought by American collectors.

Presumably Hayes knew about this codicil. It is not known what he thought of Beatty's decision. He became alarmed, however, when he received a letter from Alexis Fitzgerald stating that Beatty wished to add another codicil to his Will.[119] He wished to withdraw all his Western manuscripts from his bequest except those which were on exhibition. Fitzgerald had arranged to visit Beatty at Monte Carlo on 17 November. He asked Hayes to send him a list of the Western manuscripts which would be on exhibition at the Chester Beatty Library on that day. Hayes provided the requested list but he wondered why the manuscripts had been withdrawn. In a letter to John Wooderson, Hayes wrote: 'It is important to protect Sir Chester from any undue influence'.[120]

Beatty asked Hayes to accompany the exhibition of manuscripts to Princeton University.[121] He felt that he could not make the journey himself. The American reaction to

Beatty's manuscripts was very favourable.[122] Hayes reported that the Garrett Collection was 'poor' in comparison.[123] Beatty was no doubt as proud as he had been after his trip to the Vatican. But Hayes's report may also have compounded in Beatty's mind the view that he should do something for the country of his birth.

Beatty was weakening physically throughout his ninety-third year. His behaviour was erratic and he was easily unnerved. In March 1967 he began to worry about his complicated history of citizenship — American, British and Irish. It would surely lead to difficulties on his death and might jeopardise the future of his Library. He asked Joan O'Neill to call on Alexis Fitzgerald to convey his wish to renounce British nationality and to become a naturalised Irish citizen. He hoped that by renouncing British citizenship he would eliminate the possibility of legal proceedings in Great Britain with regard to his estate.

Fitzgerald prepared the form of Declaration of Renunciation of British Nationality but strongly advised that Beatty should retain his British citizenship.[124] There might be some unseen advantage in having it and there were no difficulties caused by its possession. As regards Beatty's desire to become a naturalised Irish citizen, Fitzgerald commented: 'I think the best I can say with regard to that is that you are in the most ample and complete manner known to Irish law already an Irish citizen'.[125]

Beatty's solicitor was satisfied that the possibility of proceedings being brought in Great Britain against Beatty's estate depended on the law of domicile. It could not be shown that Beatty's domicile was anything other than Irish. Fitzgerald was also satisfied, as Hayes had been, that under the provisions of the Succession Act, 1965: 'it would be possible to demonstrate that you had made proper provision for your children and grandchildren'.[126]

Fitzgerald discussed the matter with Hayes.[127] They decided to stall for time and Fitzgerald wrote to Beatty to say that the matter could be given full consideration when he returned to Dublin in May.[128] Hayes was perplexed and must have found it difficult to know what to write to Beatty. Unfortunately he may have inadvertently influenced Beatty

once again. He wrote with news of a sale of Armenian manuscripts at Sotheby's. The 23 manuscripts on offer were valued
at £500,000. Hayes felt that on the basis of Sotheby's esti-
mates the Chester Beatty Armenian collection would be
worth £1,500,000. 'In the light of this and other recent prices
it seems to me that your whole collection might well exceed
the ten million mark'.[129]

In April Beatty decided that he would not travel to Ireland.
He wrote:

> I have at last had to come to the sad decision that at 92
> my travelling days are over. I am feeling very well at the
> moment, but I am afraid that once there I might not be
> able to get back to the Riviera. I love Ireland and the
> Irish people and have spent some very happy years there,
> but I feel sure that I could never survive an Irish winter.[130]

Hayes was very disappointed:

> It was shattering news for all of us when we heard that
> you were not coming over on May 15th as originally
> planned. Health considerations must of course come
> first and if you do not feel able for the move to Dublin
> you are wise not to attempt it.[131]

Hayes arranged to visit Beatty at Monte Carlo on 27 June.
Beatty apologised that he would not be able to see him for
very long: 'The doctors tell me that I must not get too tired'.[132]

Hayes was no longer in control. Beatty had previously
relied on him to act as his liaison officer. Now while Beatty's
health was deteriorating, Hayes was not by his side to protect
him from rash decisions.

As Hayes returned from Monaco on 28 June, the British
and Irish newspapers reported that a brisk twenty-minute
sale at Sotheby's of ten paintings belonging to Sir Chester
Beatty had raised £242,100.[133] Beatty was amazed at the
prices paid. In a state of elation, he wrote a dramatic letter
to a New York bookdealer, H.P. Kraus. He referred to a letter
which he had received from Kraus in 1964. The bookdealer
had written: 'I am still dreaming of the day when you might
decide to sell me some of your choice Western manuscripts'.[134]

Beatty now gave Kraus every reason to believe that his day had arrived.

Kraus was a powerful bookdealer who loved to chase an important collection. In February 1957 he had visited the Chester Beatty Library and was very impressed by it. Following Merton's death later the same year, Kraus had expressed an interest in acquiring Merton's library.[135] He had been told that the sale was being handled by the London bookseller Bernard Breslauer.[136] He contacted Breslauer, who told him that the library was not for sale. Kraus was not discouraged. In 1958 he flew to London and bargained with Breslauer until he had succeeded in purchasing the best items.[137]

In his autobiography, Kraus described his contact with Beatty in a chapter titled 'My Greatest Disappointment'.[138] He claimed that Beatty had invited him to Dublin in 1959 to make an offer for the Chester Beatty Western manuscripts. Kraus wrote:

> Going through Beatty's collection was the kind of delight a bookman gets only on rare occasions and hardly ever with a private collection . . . I had no way of knowing what value he placed on the collection; undoubtedly he hoped for a good profit and deserved it, since prices had increased considerably . . . Having seen the collection I went to Cannes where Sir Chester lived at the time. I had carefully calculated the value of the collection and wanted to submit my offer.[139]

There were 76 Western manuscripts and two were outstanding in Kraus's opinion.[140] If Beatty was willing to sell 74, retaining the two important manuscripts, Kraus would pay £230,000. Beatty had asked for half an hour to consider the offer. He was smiling when he returned: 'You give me great pleasure with these figures, Kraus. You have offered me three times my cost. This is wonderful. I always thought I paid too much. Thank you, yes, thank you indeed'.[141]

Kraus was delighted and asked: 'When may I pick up the books?' He was shocked when Beatty replied:

> Oh, I'm not selling! . . . I never mentioned anything about selling . . . Oh, it's a fair offer, yes, but what

should I do with the money? I am an old man. I have oatmeal in the morning, eggs or some meat at noon and evening, not even wine. Thanks ever so much. You have made me very happy.[142]

Kraus was distinctly unhappy. He had wasted time and expense in order to give Beatty 'what amounted to a free appraisal'.

It was against this background that Kraus received Beatty's letter of 29 June 1967. Beatty wrote:

After much thought, I have now decided to sell some of my manuscripts, and I want to give you the choice of handling the sale for me, as we are such old friends, and I know you will get them good homes in the universities and museums in America, where the public will have the full benefit of seeing them . . . I suggest you go to Dublin and look over the whole collection of Western manuscripts and give me your ideas. None of them is tied up in any way, except that I have promised to make a gift to the Irish nation and I imagine I will leave them the bulk of those on exhibition . . . This matter, I think, should remain very, very confidential because the newspapers can make such a terrible lot of trouble.[143]

Without Hayes to remind him of his commitment to the Irish Government, Beatty was obviously inclined to regard his Library as his private possession. It was untrue to say that none of the Western manuscripts were 'tied up in any way'. All those on exhibition on 17 November 1966 still legally formed part of the Chester Beatty Library bequest.

Hayes knew nothing of the offer to Kraus until he received a letter from Edith Bruhl, Beatty's secretary in the South of France. Hayes had met her during his visit to Monaco and he considered that she had Beatty's best interests at heart. Miss Bruhl must have agreed to keep Hayes informed of developments. She wrote excitedly:

Hardly had the news been received of the proceeds from the sale of the pictures (£240,000), when plans were being made to sell the bulk of the Library in America through Kraus . . . It was only after a very fierce battle that I was able to get the letter to Kraus passed in its present form. It was about four times as long, with many repetitions, of course, and saying that he intended to cut down by at least half the Armenian, Persian and other collections, as they would never be seen and would certainly be sold after his death, whatever reservations were made — in fact, a long rambling letter, full of excuses for not keeping his promise. I at last managed to convince him that it was unwise, by saying that the newspapers would make a great story out of it and forget all the good he had done in the past, and I thought it was wise to act slowly.

This must be terribly upsetting for you, but I think you should know the truth, and you are probably the one person who can delay things, so I will keep you in close touch.[144]

Hayes was not just upset, he was absolutely appalled. He replied:

I have 2 very useful allies here who will be equally discreet, J.F. Hosking and Fitzg. the lawyer. We are all planning delaying actions of various kinds.[145]

He was convinced that Beatty was being encouraged to sell his collections by people who hoped to gain some of the proceeds. It was not typical of Beatty to act in an erratic and imprudent manner. Hayes was suspicious of two French ladies — the Comtesse d'Aubigny d'Esymards and Madame Giselle Bernard.[146] It was a delicate matter and he did not wish to offend Beatty. Hayes asked Bruhl 'to check on bona fides of which I am doubtful' regarding the two ladies. He was concerned that they were trying to dupe Beatty by recouping the cost of a hotel bill twice, from Bruhl in Nice and from Joan O'Neill in Dublin.[147]

Bruhl replied that she had not paid the hotel bill. She noted:

I realise your reason for asking because of something I was told by a member of the C.B. family. The two ladies are very upset and worried about the delay in

payment. They expected to have it straight away . . .
Mme. B. has had to cancel the arrangements for the purchase of an expensive apartment in Monte Carlo.[148]

It is difficult to know what was going on during the summer
of 1967. The extant correspondence offers tantalising snippets
like Bruhl's reference to something she was told by a member
of Beatty's family. Hayes and Bruhl deliberately tried to
avoid committing too much to paper. Much of their com-
munication was by telephone. Hayes was determined that the
crisis should remain a secret one. Few people knew that it
took place.[149]

H.P. Kraus was only aware that Beatty had offered him the
'choice Western manuscripts'. He wrote: 'All I can say is that
I am delighted at the prospect . . . I consider the trust you
have in me as a great privilege'.[150] Unfortunately for Kraus,
Beatty was to disappoint him once again.

Beatty asked Hayes to forward a list of 'those Western
manuscripts that we put aside to be sold. You know the ones
I mean — those early items we picked out. I have offered
some to Kraus'.[151] He was referring to the 27 manuscripts
which had been withdrawn from the Library bequest in
August 1966. He wrote to Kraus to tell him that he had
asked Hayes to set aside the items which he wished to sell.
He cautioned Kraus not to become too excited: 'There is no
great hurry about this matter, but I thought I would offer
you some items that might interest you, in view of our long
association'.[152]

It soon became clear that the items of interest to Kraus
were not the items which Beatty proposed to sell. Kraus
took Beatty at his word and forwarded a list of the manuscripts which would be of most interest to his clients, that is,
the choice of Beatty's collection. He wrote: 'I hope sincerely
that you will include many if not all of those in the selection
you are preparing'.[153] Only one of the manuscripts chosen
by Kraus was among the 27 which Beatty thought of selling.

Hayes was distraught to think that Beatty might alter the
terms of the Library bequest. As Bruhl had pointed out, it
would ruin Beatty's good name. Hayes knew that his own
reputation was also at stake. It was largely due to his manoe-

verings that the Library bequest had been negotiated in such a satisfactory manner.

Nobody knew the weight on Hayes's mind when he went to Dublin University on 12 July to be conferred an Honorary Doctor of Literature. The degree was awarded to acknowledge Hayes's achievement in completing the bibliography which had been published in 11 volumes titled *Manuscript Sources for the History of Irish Civilisation.*[154]

Perhaps in an attempt to relieve tension, Hayes wrote to Beatty to tell him of the degree from Trinity:

> As we will then have 7 doctorates between us don't you think we might go into partnership in a rheumatism clinic. Our patients will be perfectly happy even if their rheumatism gets worse provided we charge enormous fees and then double these by calling one another into consultation in every case.[155]

Beatty began to reconsider his decision to sell material from his Library. His behaviour was, to say the least, inconsistent. Kraus must have been infuriated to receive another letter from Beatty:

> I am afraid you seem to have misunderstood my letter entirely. I do not intend to sell the cream of my entire collection of Western manuscripts . . . I do not see how you got the idea that I wanted to liquidate my collection . . . I merely suggested that you might like to look over the collection and give me your ideas . . . The manuscripts which I picked out and intend selling are all in good condition and I think they are all prior to 1500 . . . I could easily have put them up for sale in London, but I should like them to go to America because there is such a scarcity there, and the museums and libraries of Europe have such vast quantities of material which is never seen. I am not needing the money and the doctors say I am good for six or seven years yet, so there is plenty of time to examine the things carefully.[156]

Hayes was pleased to hear that Beatty was becoming less inclined to sell his manuscripts. However, Hayes decided that under no circumstances should it be known that Beatty was selling manuscripts, whether or not they had been removed from the Library bequest. He proposed that Beatty's book-plate should be removed from the 27 manuscripts which had been offered to Kraus. (Plate 33).

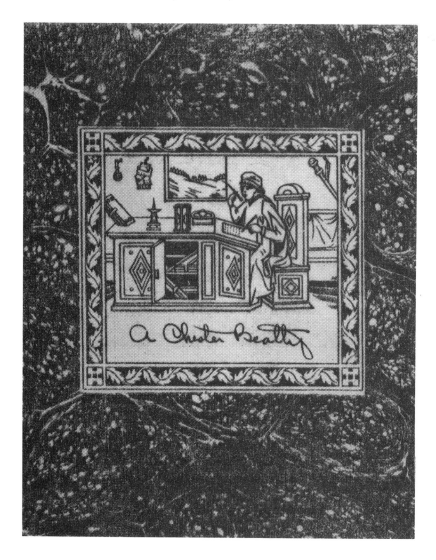

33. Beatty's bookplate (courtesy of Trustees of the CBL).

Beatty disagreed with Hayes. If the manuscripts were sold as 'from the Chester Beatty Library' they would fetch higher prices. Hayes wrote to Bruhl:

> There is much confusion of thought about this. If Kraus buys he knows they are from the Chester Beatty Library and therefore his price will not be affected. If American libraries are told by Kraus when he is selling the manuscripts are from the Chester Beatty Library, how are we to prevent big headlines in newspapers like "Great Chester Beatty Library being sold" from appearing. This would appear a natural assumption for journalists to make in view of the recent publicity for the sale of the pictures. Journalists cannot be expected to distinguish between the sale of a few unimportant manuscripts and a sale of the manuscripts in general. In any case, everyone will assume that if some are sold all will eventually be sold.[157]

Bruhl replied to Hayes that Beatty was now much calmer:

> He told me to tell you he was sorry he got so upset. He is very suspicious now, which, as you know, he has every reason to be, but unfortunately he suspects the wrong people!

> It is difficult to know what to say about removing the notes or bookplates from the books he proposes to sell, as one day he says one thing and the next day another. I do not think there is any need to hurry, as he is now talking of doing it in the next couple of years or so. Time is, of course, the great factor.

> He has rather turned against Kraus now, as he was far too eager and wanted all the best manuscripts, and Sir Chester's first letter did, in fact, rather suggest that. I dread to think what would have happened if I had sent the letter he dictated – he was offering practically the whole library! He gets very angry if I try to prevent his signing things, and if I don't he says afterwards, when he has changed his mind, "People should not let me sign things when they know I am not normal."

> The Riviera is having its hottest summer for eight years, which is not making things easier.[158]

Beatty had never before endured a hot summer in the South of France. He was fortunate that Miss Bruhl was such a shrewd and forceful lady. Hayes appreciated her efforts and dreaded to think that Beatty might have another period of 'abnormality'. In August 1967, Hayes retired from his post as Director of the National Library. The *Sunday Press* reported that he wished to devote more time to his activities at the Chester Beatty Library.[159] This was nearer the truth than they could have imagined.

Hayes decided to prepare detailed notes setting out the principal arguments against proposals to alter the terms of the Chester Beatty Library bequest.[160] These notes show the depth of Hayes's concern. Beatty had stated, verbally and in writing, that he was presenting his Library to the Irish people. He had been effusively thanked by the Irish Government. He could not change his mind without leaving himself open to the charge that his actions were dishonourable. Hayes argued:

> It would be said, and with justification, that he was not a "man of his word". In such circumstances his many other acts of generosity in the past would be quickly forgotten. It would be said that he cleverly fooled the Government in order to get various privileges. The Government has been approached on two occasions to alter legislation to suit his interests ... As it stands today the Chester Beatty Library is one of the greatest memorials to one of the greatest collectors of manuscripts of all time. If you cut away 40 or 50 per cent of the memorial, what is left is a memorial to the greatest sabotage of a collection on record.[161]

Hayes privately expressed a wish for Beatty's death.[162] He hoped that Fitzgerald would prevent Beatty from altering his Will. The solicitor had to advise Hayes:

> You will appreciate that my duty is simply to ascertain what are my client's wishes with regard to his Will and if

146

I am satisfied that he has a disposing mind which is being freely exercised, I must make it for him, even though I might disapprove on general grounds of the change.[163]

By October Hayes's state of panic had been abated. Beatty wrote to Kraus that he had decided not to sell any manuscripts: 'I think the best thing is to forget it . . . In a few years from now, if I am still here and you would still like to have them, you might let me know and we can discuss it again'.[164]

Hayes was relieved but he felt sorry for Kraus, who had been unfairly misled and shoddily treated. He wrote to the bookdealer and explained that Beatty had withdrawn most of his Western manuscripts from the Library bequest. They would be sold after his death as part of his personal estate. Hayes noted: 'Anything I can do to have them sold to you will be done'.[165]

The secret crisis was not quite finished. Hayes was perturbed to receive an order from Beatty to send some French books from his Library to one of the two ladies who had been suspected of exerting 'undue influence'. Nevertheless, he did as he had been instructed and sent 16 books to the Comtesse d'Aubigny d'Esymards.[166]

In early December, Bruhl wrote to Hayes:

I must be frank and tell you that he [Beatty] has had rather a chip on his shoulder lately about Ireland, but I have at last, I think, really convinced him that you would not do anything contrary to his wishes when he made his Will, and now his attitude seems to have changed completely and *you* are very much in favour again. But you must realise that while I am fighting for Ireland (and therefore his good name), other people are fighting against it, and occasionally he gets angry with me and tells me not to talk damn rot! Another time he will say, "You are absolutely right; I know I can always rely on your judgement". It is difficult to know where one is with him. He changes so quickly and so often . . . Between ourselves, he had a slight stroke (the result of another upset by you know whom) when I was with him on Friday. His face became terribly distorted and he could not speak for a while and looked at me as though he had never seen me before. The doctor called it a "facial spasm". It did not affect the heart but I think it was fairly serious. His face is back to normal now.[167]

On 12 December, Beatty wrote his last letter to Hayes. As if the crisis had not happened, he wrote contentedly: 'I am so glad that everything is working out so well in connection with the Library'.[168] Hayes had succeeded in convincing him that the future of the Library was secure.

Alfred Chester Beatty died at the Princess Grace Clinic in Monte Carlo on 19 January 1968, three weeks before his ninety-third birthday and exactly 11 years after he had been awarded Honorary Irish Citizenship. Although the events of 1967 had brought a turbulent end to his association with his Library and with his librarian, no lasting damage had been done and the newspapers never heard a word. Instead, Beatty's remains were returned to Ireland to receive a State Funeral to Glasnevin Cemetery in Dublin. In this final act of tribute, the Irish Government acknowledged the magnificent gift of the Chester Beatty Library.

Chapter 6

The Legacy and the Lesson

Beside a library, how poor are all the other greatest deeds of men.

Thomas Davis

Sir Alfred Chester Beatty's remains were received at Dublin Airport on 25 January 1968. After a short ceremony, at which the President, the Taoiseach and the Government were represented, the cortège drove to 10 Ailesbury Road. In a sign of growing religious maturity, members of four religious orders of nuns kept vigil before the remains were removed to St Patrick's Cathedral.[1]

The State Funeral took place on 29 January. The funeral service was conducted by the Dean of St Patrick's Cathedral, Very Rev. J.W. Armstrong, and presided over by Most Rev. Dr G.O. Simms. In a panegyric, Dr Simms acclaimed 'a prince among benefactors ... a philanthropist, a patron of the arts, an industrialist who became a world figure, and a lover of Ireland'.[2]

The occasion was a memorable one in the history of the State. Hitherto the honour of a State Funeral had been reserved for patriots, statesmen and soldiers. Beatty was the first person born outside the State to receive the honour and he received the gesture as a champion of culture. It was also the first time the President and Taoiseach had participated, in their official capacities, at a Protestant funeral service.[3]

Beatty's grave at Glasnevin Cemetery is marked by a simple

149

block of Irish granite. (Plate 34). He would not have wished for a more elaborate monument. His memorial is to be found elsewhere in Dublin — at 20 Shrewsbury Road.

34. Beatty's grave, Glasnevin Cemetery, Dublin.

When the details of Beatty's Will were announced, the *Irish Press* proudly asserted 'Sir Alfred keeps word to nation'.[4] Beatty's assets in Ireland were valued at £7,075,608. Of this amount, £6 million was attributable to the Chester Beatty Library and its contents. This was, of course, a gross underestimate and the true value of the Library is incalculable. Dr Hayes stated the case more correctly when he said: 'The coming of the Library to Ireland was the greatest cultural event of the century'.[5] Few Irish people have even begun to realise the national asset which Sir Chester Beatty entrusted to them. (Plates 35 and 36).

The Library contains representative art collections from many civilisations. It is an antidote to insularity and isolationism in a small island country. Beatty provided Irish people and their foreign visitors with an unrivalled opportunity to become acquainted with other cultures, languages, religions, art forms and techniques. He contributed to the broadening of attitudes and the expansion of horizons. The Library is an outstanding international art collection which nobly compliments Ireland's renowned national collections.

The potential of the Chester Beatty Library is clearly vast. It awaits recognition from the Irish people who pay for its upkeep. The process of increasing public awareness has begun and the Library is becoming more than 'a flower in the Government's buttonhole'. It still provides an ideal setting in which to entertain distinguished visitors to Ireland but its importance as an educational and cultural facility is beginning to emerge.

Beatty's additions to the Irish cultural heritage encompassed the gifts to the National Gallery of Ireland, the gift of Oriental weaponry to the Curragh Camp Military Museum, and the gift of the Chester Beatty Library. But the psychological impact of his presence in the country must also be acknowledged. He was a focus of attention because of his cultural gifts. He provided good reason for cultural affairs to be discussed at meetings of the Irish Government.

Irish political leaders gratefully acknowledged Beatty's munificence. They had done everything they could to offer him a pleasant retirement home. Beatty had received honours in return for his gifts. In a tribute, President de Valera said:

These acts on our part were but tokens of our deep appreciation of the riches he has given to our land. The name of Chester Beatty will continue to be mentioned with gratitude by future generations in this island, which

151

he chose as his home and the object of a noble-minded patronage and which he has now chosen to be the resting place of his mortal remains.[6]

The Taoiseach, Mr Lynch, said that Beatty was 'a munificent benefactor and friend of our country'. His predecessors also remembered Beatty's 'abiding interest in Ireland's welfare'.[7]

The newspapers followed the Government in offering tribute to Chester Beatty. All four daily newspapers in the Republic of Ireland devoted editorials to 'the most munificent patron of recent years'.[8] There were lengthy obituaries in British newspapers recalling the achievements of the 'philanthropic millionaire and art collector'.[9]

The conditions of Beatty's Will were fulfilled according to his wishes. Arrangements were made for the President and the Taoiseach to appoint one member each to the Board of Trustees of the Chester Beatty Library. The Attorney General advised that legislation would be necessary to enable the President to exercise this power.[10] An appropriate Bill was drafted and introduced in the Seanad on 24 April 1968. As the Bill passed its second and subsequent stages in the Dáil on 9 May, the Taoiseach and other politicians once again took the opportunity to deliver tributes to Chester Beatty.[11]

The Chester Beatty Library was formally handed over to the Board of Trustees on 9 September 1968. President de Valera must have derived satisfaction from the occasion. He presented the Deeds of Trust to the Chairman of the Board of Trustees, Dr Hayes.[12] (Plate 37).

On 26 July 1975, de Valera's successor as President, Cearbhall Ó Dálaigh, had the pleasure of honouring the promise which he had helped to secure from the Government, when he formally opened an extension to the Chester Beatty Library. (Plate 38). In his address, President Ó Dálaigh said that the real value of the Library was the use which Ireland proposed to make of it. He explained:

My personal hope is that, while of course this great collection is open to experts and scholars from all over the world, the means will be found, by fellowships and kindred devices, to attract (among others) young Irishmen and women into this world of fascinating beauty

152

35. *Japanese Print by Kunisada (1786-1864) 'A Servant holding his Master's armour' (courtesy of Trustees of the CBL).*

153

36. Chinese carved red lacquer panel showing three Taoist immortals and a stork, the symbol of longevity, in a root-wood boat. The beggar Immortal, Li T'ieh-kuai, sits astride his gourd. Ch'ien-lung period, 1736-95.

and mystery which the western world has cared too little about.

In down-to-earth language, I would hope that our Universities will build up small but learned faculties to explore and exploit this great collection. It may be that in the nature of university structures, this development will have to come in the form of an Institute or Institutes, university-integrated; as I feel that an appeal, in foreign parts, for the necessary wherewithal for these purposes could succeed only if made by a specific Institute and in respect of a well-defined area or areas of study.

At another level, I hope the now extended Library will

37. The handing over of the Chester Beatty Library to the Board of Trustees, 9 September 1968.
L. to R.: Jack Lynch (Taoiseach), R.P. Hayes, Eamon de Valera (President), and James Hosking.

155

also find the modest means required for *haute vulgarisation*, or popularisation, which should go hand in hand with serious scholarship.[13]

It is to be hoped that the Irish Government will consider President Ó Dálaigh's appeal for further financial investment in the Chester Beatty Library. While the founder was alive, the Government assured him that his Library would be gratefully received. It was a magnificent gift but one which carried much responsibility. The upkeep of a major art collection involves adequate conservation facilities. The exploitation of the collection calls for bursaries, fellowships and suitable study libraries. The display of the collection demands appropriate lighting, heating, and security. Publicity implies the cost of advertising, publishing and travelling exhibitions.

38. The new Gallery — Chester Beatty Library — opened 26 July 1975. (Extension to the exhibition gallery opened in August 1957 — see plate 25).

156

These are short-term needs. The Government can continue its admirable record of co-operation with the wishes of Sir Chester Beatty by answering them. The lesson of enlightened cultural politics has not been exhausted.

In their treatment of Sir Chester Beatty, the Irish Government brought about a major advance in cultural policy. Their action was prompt and salutary. Whatever about the general state of cultural awareness, a satisfactory solution was found in this case. Eamon de Valera deserves special mention. While he admitted that he did not have much experience of the type of art on view at the Chester Beatty Library, he showed himself to be very experienced in human relations. He enjoyed Beatty's company and was determined that he should be treated sympathetically.[14] It is indeed pleasing to commend the politicians from all parties who helped to secure the future of these splendid collections.

The lesson for the future of Irish cultural politics is that similar wealthy and benevolent individuals can be encouraged to settle in the country. The Government must be willing to pay for the prestige and privilege of acquiring the domicile of such people. The possibility of acquiring important gifts in return for considerate treatment provides a relatively easy and inexpensive means of increasing the cultural heritage of the nation.

The case of Chester Beatty and Ireland also highlights the role of senior civil servants. Frederick Boland's report of his meeting with Beatty in June 1949 was sufficiently influential to encourage a warm reception from politicians. They were amateurs in the world of cultural politics, while Beatty proved to be an expert. Irish bureaucracy showed admirable flexibility – an important instance of enlightened cultural administrative practice.

Beatty's impact as a cultural benefactor must not be ignored. He pushed the Irish Government into acknowledging a role for the arts – everything from bookbinding to Persian miniatures. He was positive in all that he said. Seán T. O'Kelly and Eamon de Valera undoubtedly recognised that Beatty had great leadership qualities. They admired his drive and enthusiasm, his will to see things done. While Beatty used his influence as discreet pressure, his motivation was largely generous promotion of the arts in the public interest. If he sought immortality like many another wealthy man, it was a permissible act of self-interest. Perhaps in old age he felt the need to redistribute the vast fortune which he had earned from his efforts as an industrialist. It was fortunate for Ireland that Beatty chose Dublin as his retirement home. Few nations have received a gift like the Chester Beatty Library, one which demands to be seen. It is hoped that the Library will live and grow as the legacy of a friend and patron of Ireland.

Notes

NOTES TO CHAPTER 1 (pp 15-19)

1 For an account of this policy, see Margaret O'Callaghan, 'Language and Religion: the quest for identity in the Irish Free State' (unpublished M.A. Thesis, University College, Dublin, 1981).

2 Terence Brown, *Ireland — a Social and Cultural History 1922-79* (London, 1981), p. 148. This is the first serious attempt to examine the subject. The absence of references to Irish cultural history in general histories is often surprising. There has been a preoccupation with political history and a severe neglect of the cultural development of Ireland since 1922.

3 Thomas Bodkin, *A Report on the Arts in Ireland* (Dublin, 1949), p. 8.

4 Maurice Moynihan (ed.), *Speeches and Statements by Eamon de Valera, 1917-73* (Dublin, 1980), p. 233.

5 E.g. John A. Costello's speech to the first meeting of the Arts Council, quoted *Irish Press*, 26 Jan. 1952.

6 *Irish Press*, 5 Sept. 1931.

7 *Irish Independent*, 12 Aug. 1954.

8 *Report on the Arts*, p. 28.

9 *Irish Times*, 10 Aug. 1953. After studying the exhibits at the Chester Beatty Library on the day of its opening, de Valera said: 'As you know, I have not much experience in these matters'. A similar admission appears in a letter from John L. Burke to John A. Costello (SPO S 14559A; 10 June 1950): 'I spoke to Mr de Valera some time ago on how starved culturally our city is, and he admitted in all humility that he was to blame'.

10 TCD MS 8133(55); Beatty to Thomas McGreevy, 23 Apr. 1958.

11 P. & G. Ford, *Select List of Reports and Inquiries of the Irish Dáil and Senate, 1920-1972* (Dublin, 1974), pp 53-4.

12 SPO S 14922A; 21 Feb. 1951.

NOTES TO CHAPTER 2 (pp 20-40)

1 See Appendices A & B, pp 00 to 00.

2 CBP; notes of Robert Chetwood Beatty, 17 Feb. 1894.

3 Armagh Cathedral Library; MSS of the late Very Rev. H.W. Ren-

159

nison. The assistance of the Keeper, Rev. J. Crook, is gratefully acknowledged.

4   CBP; Douglas Leffingwell to William Gedney Beatty, 1 Dec. 1924.

5   CBP; Robert W. Beatty to Wm. Gedney Beatty, 24 Jan. 1894.

6   CBP; Beatty's unpublished memoirs, p. 1.

7   Columbia University Archive; the author is grateful to Mr Paul Palmer and Ms Leonore F. Bona for their help in locating a copy of Beatty's examination record.

8   T.A. Rickard (1864-1953) was born in Italy, reared in Russia, educated in England, and had gained mining experience in Australia and North America. His father was Cornish and his mother Scots-Irish. In later life he became a leading mining historian and one of the founders of mining journalism.

9   Mark Wyman, *Hard Rock Epic* (Berkeley, California, 1979), p. 46.

10   T.A. Rickard, *Interviews with Mining Engineers* (San Francisco, 1922).

11   For an excellent study of mining magnates like Beatty, see Richard H. Peterson, *The Bonanza Kings: Social Origins and Business Behaviour of Western Mining Entrepreneurs, 1870-1910* (Lincoln, Nebraska, 1977).

12   Hammond (1855-1936) was Cecil Rhodes's chief engineer in South Africa. He was later based in London for a few years before returning to the United States in 1901. When he offered Beatty the job as his assistant the young engineer replied: 'I still have beer tastes, though I hope to get to champagne some day'. See *The Autobiography of John Hays Hammond* (New York, 1935), p. 483.

13   CBP; Beatty to Herbert Hoover, 26 Dec. 1911. After a long legal battle, Beatty finally won the case in 1918 and received compensation worth $27,300 and the right to disputed shares in a Yukon goldmine.

14   *Mining Magazine* 7 (Nov. 1912), pp 326-8, article by the editor, T.A. Rickard, 'A New Group'.

15   An excellent biography of Hoover (1874-1964), with much information about Beatty, is being researched by George H. Nash. Part One has already been published, *The Life of Herbert Hoover: The Engineer, 1874-1914* (New York, 1983).

16   Beatty's first wife was the cousin and sister-in-law of T.A. Rickard. His daughter Ninette (1901-62) married Captain Edward Newling and had one child, Anne (1930-). His son Alfred Chester (1907-83) was married three times and had one child by his first marriage, a daughter, Sarah (1934-).

17   Baroda House is now the residence of the Saudi Arabian Ambassador to the Court of St James.

18   Edith Dunn (1888-1952) was an Irish-American Catholic whose parents came from Dobb's Ferry, where Chester Beatty went to school. In 1907 she married Carol Dater Stone but they were

divorced after a few years. She married Beatty in London on 21 June 1913.

19 During their first winters in Egypt the Beattys lived in a mansion called Bait el Abyad (the White House). Later they built to their own design a magnificent villa, Bait el Azrak (the Blue House), situated at Mena some miles from Cairo and in the shadow of the Great Pyramid.

20 On 16 March 1981, Selection Trust became a wholly owned subsidiary of British Petroleum, having been bought out the previous summer at a cost of £412 million, the largest takeover bid in the history of the City of London.

21 CBP; Catalogue of Chinese Snuff Bottles, dated 2 March 1914 and listing 1,674 items.

22 Interview with Jack Hillier, 25 May 1984.

23 *The Times*, 19 Nov. 1931.

24 British Museum; Standing Committee Minute Books, 1923-63.

25 Victoria and Albert Museum; Chester Beatty Files, 1923-58.

26 Sir Malcolm Watson, *African Highway: The Battle for Health in Central Africa* (London, 1953).

27 *British Bulletin of Commerce* (War-Time Trading Bulletin), No. 109, 'The United Kingdom Commercial Corporation Survey 1940-44'.

28 CBP; Beatty to Wilfred Merton, 31 May 1940. The setback referred to was the evacuation of troops from Dunkirk following the surrender of the Belgian army.

29 For the Cairo Conference (22-26 Nov. 1943), see Winston Churchill, *The Second World War* (London, 1952), Vol. V, p. 280, and also Harold Macmillan, *The Blast of War, 1939-45* (London, 1967), pp 430-1.

30 For an entertaining description of Beatty's war-time activities, see Arthur Wilson, *The Life and Times of Sir Alfred Chester Beatty* (London, 1985), pp 227-53. This is a useful popular biography which emphasises Beatty's career as a mining engineer. Unfortunately the chapters regarding Beatty's years in Ireland repeat many stories which owe more to myth than to reality. The biography suffers greatly because Wilson has not quoted Beatty's letters.

31 CBP; Beatty to Colonel D.K.E. Bruce, 23 Apr. 1945.

NOTES TO CHAPTER 3 (pp 41-64)

1 The Labour Party won 393 seats (of a total 640), including 79 seats which had never before returned a Labour M.P.

2 H.C.Deb., 5S., Vol. 417, Cols 425-6.

3 Quoted in Harry Hopkins, *The New Look: A Social History of the Forties and Fifties in Britain* (London, 1963), pp 27-8.

4 Beatty had not had much opportunity to exercise his voting pre-

ference. He became a naturalised British citizen in 1933 and there had only been one general election in Great Britain between 1933 and 1945. This was in June 1935 when Stanley Baldwin led the Conservative Party to victory. It is not possible to ascertain if Beatty was a member of the Conservative Party or if he gave financial support. Such details are held to be confidential. The assistance of Mr T.J. Hollins of the Conservative Research Department is gratefully acknowledged.

5　*The Times*, 8 Feb. 1965.

6　Michael Foot, *Aneurin Bevan 1945-60* (London, 1973), pp 237-44.

7　Retirement dinner 27 Sept. 1950. The author is grateful to Mr Cyril Kidd of Selection Trust Ltd. (now retired) for his help in locating a copy of this speech.

8　*Sunday Express*, 6 Nov. 1949.

9　Sheila Wingfield, *Sun Too Fast* (London, 1974), pp 217-44.

10　A.J. Wilson, *Life of Beatty*, p. 264.

11　The Republic of Ireland's currency retained one-to-one parity with sterling until March 1979.

12　Ronan Fanning, *The Irish Department of Finance, 1922-58* (Dublin, 1978), p. 475.

13　Interviews with Mr Basil Gray (1 June 1984), Mr B.W. Robinson (29 May 1984), Mr Robert Skelton (24 May 1984), Professor William Watson (26 May 1984), and Dr Patrick Henchy (2 Feb. 1984).

14　Sir Ronald Prain, *Reflections on an Era: Fifty Years of Mining in Changing Africa* (London, 1981), p. 88. The rate of exchange of sterling was devalued against the American dollar by 30.5% from $4.03 to $2.80.

15　Hopkins, *The New Look*, p. 454.

16　*Irish Times*, 7 Sept. 1950.

17　*Daily Telegraph*, 10 July 1956.

18　*Sunday Express*, 6 Nov. 1949.

19　*Reflections on an Era*, pp 90-1.

20　CBP; Beatty to Colonel Bruce, 15 Nov. 1945.

21　Wilson, *Life of Beatty*, p. 264.

22　CBP; Beatty to Colonel Bruce, 15 Nov. 1945.

23　CBP; Beatty to Bodmer, 17 Apr. 1946. For an entertaining description of Bodmer, a shy, serious and complex character (quite the opposite to Beatty), see H.P. Kraus, *A Rare Book Saga* (London, 1979), pp 277-88. See also *Who's Who in Switzerland*, 1964/65 (Geneva, 1964).

24　CBP; Bodmer to Beatty, 26 Apr. 1946.

25　CBP; Beatty to Bodmer, 2 May 1946.

26　In August 1946 Beatty paid £10,000 on Bodmer's behalf for a number of manuscripts at the Phillipps sale at Sotheby's. By October Bodmer was able to repay the money and thanked Beatty profusely.

27　CBP; Beatty to Wilkinson, Oct. 1946.

28 A number of people interviewed by the author have said that Edith Beatty had a severe drink problem at this time. Her husband went to London in June 1951 for their wedding anniversary but they lived apart after 1947.

29 H.C.Deb., 5S., 431, 2306 (Mr Quentin Hogg, M.P., Oxford), 19 Dec. 1946.

30 *Ibid.*, 2307.

31 *Ibid.*, 2312-3.

32 See Vincent Grogan, *The Principles and Practices of Irish Income Tax* (Dublin, 1952), pp 185-94.

33 For the Irish tax rates, see Grogan, *ibid.*, pp 334-5 and 368-70. Information about British tax rates is found in *Simon's Taxes* (3rd edition, London, 1976), Vol. A, pp 262-77 and 281-2.

34 CBP, Beatty to Wilkinson, 10 Nov. 1953.

35 *Ibid.*, 29 Dec. 1946. Wilkinson (1885-1957) joined the Department of Oriental Manuscripts and Printed Books in 1924 after spending 13 years in the Indian Civil Service.

36 *Ibid.*

37 CBP; Beatty to Wilkinson, 24 Feb. 1947.

38 *Ibid.*, 5 Apr. 1947. It should be noted that Beatty's frustration did not stop him from continuing to support the British Museum. In July 1948 he gave some of his biblical papyri on loan to the Museum for the 'Exhibition of Biblical Manuscripts and Early Printed Editions of the Bible'. Beatty blamed Sir John Forsdyke for allowing bureaucracy to invade what he regarded as the greatest museum in the world.

39 CBP; Beatty to Arthur Arberry, 4 Jan. 1950.

40 CBP; Beatty to Wilkinson, 22 Oct. 1953.

41 *Ibid.*, 11 Apr. 1947.

42 CBP; Wilkinson to Wooderson, 6 Dec. 1948.

43 *The Times*, 8 Feb. 1965.

44 *Irish Tatler and Sketch*, May 1956.

45 Shelbourne Hotel Register, 30 Aug. 1937. The author is grateful to the manager of the Shelbourne Hotel for his assistance.

46 Interview with Joan O'Neill, 23 Feb. 1984.

47 CBP; 10 Dec. 1945.

48 For a description of Mount Armstrong, see Mark Bence-Jones, *Burke's Guide to Country Houses*, Vol. I, Ireland (London, 1978), p. 212.

49 CBP; Beatty to Wilkinson, 20 June 1949.

50 F.S.L. Lyons, *Ireland Since the Famine* (London, paperback edn., 1973), p. 593.

51 Ronan Fanning, *Independent Ireland* (Dublin, 1983), p. 169.

52 SPO S 14856A.

53 *Ibid.*, Boland was incorrect in stating that two of Beatty's grandfathers were of Irish origin.

54 *Ibid.*

55 *Ibid.*, 29 June, 1950.

56 SPO S 15345A; 21 June 1952.
57 CBP; Jean Marsh to Emery Walker Ltd., 21 June 1949.
58 CBP; 11 Oct. 1949.
59 CBP; 5 Aug. 1949.
60 CBP; 7 Aug. 1949.
61 CBP; 1 Dec. 1949.
62 Maurice Moynihan, *Currency and Central Banking in Ireland, 1922-1960* (Dublin, 1975), pp 536-7.
63 CBP; Wilkinson to Beatty, 25 Jan. 1950.
64 CBP; 8 Nov. 1949.
65 CBP; 16 Dec. 1949. Under the British Museum Act 1753, the three Principal Trustees were: the Archbishop of Canterbury, the Lord Chancellor and the Speaker of the House of Commons. In practice, the Archbishop acted as Principal Trustee. The British Museum Act, 1963, reconstituted the governing structure by establishing a Board of Trustees, 25 in number, one of whom was elected Chairman.
66 Forsdyke's successor, Thomas Kendrick, was a personal friend of Wilkinson. A kindly and popular Director (1950-9), he was quite a contrast to Forsdyke. For brief biographies of the two Directors, see *British Museum Society Bulletin* No. 33, March 1980, pp 32-3.
67 CBP; 26 Apr. 1950.
68 CBP; 22 Dec. 1949.
69 CBP; 3 Jan. 1950.
70 CBP, 17 Jan. 1950.
71 CBP; 29 Dec. 1949.
72 CBP; Wilkinson to Arberry, 16 Jan. 1950.
73 Shelbourne Hotel Registers, 1939-45.
74 *Irish Times*, 7 Sept. 1950.
75 James Meenan, *The Irish Economy since 1922* (Liverpool, 1970), p. 209. Immigration figures are difficult to determine. In 1946 the number of residents in the Twenty-six Counties who were born outside it was 98,000, and of these, 49,000 were born in Great Britain and 33,500 in the Six Counties. The figures for 1961 are, respectively, 98,951, 54,000 and 27,129. In the 1951 census the number of questions asked was insufficient to produce figures regarding foreign-born residents.
76 *Sunday Review*, 2 Sept. 1962.
77 David O'Mahony, *The Irish Economy: An Introductory Description* (Cork, 1964), p. 4.
78 *Sunday Dispatch*, 10 Sept. 1950.
79 *Irish Times*, 7 Sept. 1950.
80 *Dáil Debates*, Vol. 117, Col. 1370; 20 July 1949.
81 *Dáil Debates*, Vol. 125, Col. 1288; 24 Apr. 1951.

NOTES TO CHAPTER 4 (pp 65-107)

1 Quoted in Charles Lysaght, *Brendan Bracken* (London, 1979), p. 312. In 1958 Beatty contributed £1,000 to a memorial fund to provide a reading room in the library of Churchill College, Cambridge, which would be named after Bracken.
2 D/Ex A file No. 338/316; 24 Sept. 1949.
3 *Ibid.*, note of L.T. McCauley, 24 Sept. 1949.
4 CBP; Wilkinson to Arberry, 8 Mar. 1950.
5 CBP; 2 Apr. 1950.
6 The site had formed part of the gardens of the Church of Ireland Archbishop of Dublin's residence.
7 D/Ex A 338/316; 31 July 1950.
8 *Ibid.*, M. Mooney to Dr Nolan, 31 July 1950.
9 SPO S 14856A; 4 Aug. 1950.
10 D/Ex A 338/316; 4 Aug. 1950.
11 *The Chester Beatty Collection* (Dublin, July 1950).
12 SPO CAB G.C. 5/188, Item 4; 4 July 1950.
13 SPO S 14856A; 5 July 1950. Joan O'Neill (Beatty's business secretary in Dublin, 1950-68) told the author (interview 3 Apr. 1984) that when Beatty received this letter he was at first confused. He asked Miss O'Neill, 'Who is this John A. Costello and what does the word "taoiseach" mean?' He was delighted to be told that the letter of thanks came from the Irish Prime Minister.
14 *Ibid.*, 6 July 1950.
15 *Ibid.*, 6 Sept. 1950.
16 *Ibid.* Costello's speech was based on a draft by Thomas McGreevy which had been amended by Dr N.G. Nolan.
17 SPO S 14559A; 28 Nov. 1949.
18 SPO S 14856B; 11 Sept. 1950. The dinner was attended by the Lord Mayor of Dublin (Alfie Byrne); the Earl of Rosse (President of the Friends of the National Collections); Rt Rev. Mgr Boylan; Prof. J.G. Nolan (President of the Royal Irish Academy); Frederick Boland; Thomas McGreevy; Rt Rev. Mgr Kissane (President of Maynooth College); General Richard Mulcahy (Minister for Education); Seán MacBride (Minister for External Affairs); W.E.D. Allen; and Seán Keating (President of the Royal Hibernian Academy).
19 SPO S 14559A; 9 Aug. 1950.
20 *The Leader*, 7 Oct. 1950, article headlined 'The Beatty Collection'.
21 *The Irish Review and Annual*, 1950, article titled 'National Gallery is given fine collection by millionaire donor'.
22 Forty-five of the 93 pictures were to form a permanent exhibition at the National Gallery and the others were given on loan to galleries in Dublin, Cork, Limerick, Kilkenny, Clonmel, Waterford, Drogheda and Galway.
23 *Irish Press*, 11 July 1950.
24 *Evening Herald*, 11 July 1950.

25 *Ibid.*, repeated the following day, *Irish Independent*, 12 July 1950.
26 Other examples include: *Irish Press*, 26 Jan. 1957, *Cork Examiner*, 25 Jan. 1968, *Evening Herald*, 20 Jan. 1968.
27 *Irish Independent*, 8 Nov. 1965.
28 Glasnevin Cemetery Records. Burial plot SD 52 & 53a 11 & 54½ South New Chapel. The author is grateful to Mr B. Quinn for his assistance.
29 D/Ex A 338/316; 23 Aug. 1950.
30 *Ibid.*, 5 Sept. 1950.
31 *Ibid.*, 13 Sept. 1950.
32 *Ibid.*
33 CBP; 20 Oct. 1950.
34 CBP; 27 Oct. 1950.
35 CBP; 17 Nov. 1950.
36 *The Chester Beatty Biblical Papyri* (Dublin, 1950).
37 TCD Register's Office; the citation noted Beatty's contribution to mine engineering, his magnificent art collections and his advancement of biblical scholarship.
38 National University of Ireland, Registrar's Office; the citation intimated the eagerness with which Irish scholars awaited the completion of Beatty's Library at Shrewsbury Road.
39 *Irish Independent*, 10 Oct. 1950.
40 SPO S 14856A; McGreevy to Mr Foley, 17 Aug. 1950. In December 1957 Beatty allowed Mgr Kissane to show 29 biblical papyri on exhibition at Maynooth College Library. He also presented a gift to Maynooth of two lots of Papal Bulls and a volume of letters regarding a Jesuit mission in China.
41 CBP; 7 Oct. 1951.
42 Royal Irish Academy, Dawson Street, Secretary's records.
43 SPO S 15073A.
44 *Ibid.*, memorandum 'The Arts in Ireland' by P.J. Little, 22 Oct. 1951.
45 *Ibid.*, 30 Nov. 1951.
46 *Ibid.*, 4 Dec. 1951.
47 *Irish Times*, 29 Aug. 1962.
48 Letter of Mervyn Wall (Secretary of the Arts Council, 1957-75) to the author, 31 July 1984. The Minute books of meetings of the Arts Council do not record what members said, only decisions made.
49 *Irish Independent*, 26 Sept. 1953.
50 CBP, Wilkinson to Beatty, 24 Apr. 1952.
51 The house, 'St Margarets', is now the Teresian School. Merton (1888-1957) was the business partner of Sir Emery Walker in the publishing firm Emery Walker Ltd. A book collector and manuscripts expert, Merton was responsible for the publication of Beatty's catalogues from 1927 to 1957.
52 James Hosking (died 1981) first met Beatty in January 1931. As

manager of Lloyd's Bank in Moorgate, he had organised a small exhibition of mineral samples. Beatty, whose office was nearby, noticed the exhibition and was interested to meet the person who had arranged it. The meeting with Hosking went so well that over the next few weeks he received Beatty's personal account, the accounts of seven of his companies and those of most of his staff! Hosking's house in Dublin was at Frascati Park, Blackrock.

53 Miss Dyson (died 1974) had worked for Zaehnsdorf & Co. in London, where Beatty had admired her expertise. An elderly Cockney, she was unenthusiastic about moving to Dublin. In 1957 she relented when Beatty bought her a house at 29 Trimleston Gardens, Booterstown.

54 Wilkinson's choice of books rather limited his perspective. He bought Constantia Maxwell's *Country and Town in Ireland under the Georges*, Honor Tracy's *Mind You I've Said Nothing*, and Elizabeth Bowen's *The Shelbourne*.

55 CBP; Wilkinson to Arberry, 29 Mar. 1956.

56 D/Ex A 338/316; 8 Aug. 1952.

57 *Ibid.*

58 *Sunday Press*, 9 Aug. 1953.

59 *Irish Press* and *Irish Times*, 25 Sept. 1953.

60 The collection had been catalogued by Basil Robinson of the Department of Metals, Victoria & Albert Museum. In his opinion the collection was 'a remarkable one — not so much for containing anything of surprising uniqueness, but because of its representative character and the variety of good things which it comprises' (Wilkinson to Joan O'Neill, 16 Apr. 1952). It included early firearms, swords, knives, daggers and axes from India, Turkey, Afghanistan, Japan, Siam and the Congo.

61 *Irish Press*, 25 Sept. 1953.

62 CBP; Beatty to A.J. Collins, 27 Aug. 1953.

63 UCD A; McGilligan Papers, 6 Sept. 1955.

64 The Friends of the National Collections of Ireland was founded in 1924 by Sarah Purser. Its primary aim was to campaign for the restoration of the Lane pictures from the National Gallery, London. See below, pp 82-4.

65 See above, Chapter 3, p. 58.

66 NGI CB 1951; 1 Dec. 1951.

67 CBP; Witt to Wilkinson, 24 Apr. 1951.

68 CBP; Beatty to Wilkinson, 5 Mar. 1952.

69 *Guide to the Irish Manuscripts exhibited in the Library of Trinity College Dublin* (Dublin, 1953).

70 *Evening Herald*, 28 Apr. 1953.

71 *Irish Press*, 27 Apr. 1953. The quote is from Mr de Valera's speech at the closing of An Tóstal in Ennis.

72 CBP; Beatty to Wilkinson, 18 Feb. 1955. He had purchased five volumes for £30.

73 CBP; Beatty to Wilkinson, 21 Nov. 1955.

74 CBP; Beatty to Merton, 20 Nov. 1953. By 1958 he had acquired 57 Jesuit Relations ranging in date from 1566 to 1736.

75 Sheila Wingfield in a letter to the author, 22 Feb. 1984.

76 Interview with Joan O'Neill, 23 Feb. 1984.

77 *Irish Independent*, 10 June 1954.

78 *Dublin Evening Mail*, 6 July 1954, and *Irish Independent*, 7 July 1954.

79 *Irish Independent*, 12 Aug. 1954. The Library was to be opened to the public on Wednesday afternoon.

80 SPO S 15749.

81 *Irish Press*, 1 Oct. 1954.

82 Sir Hugh Lane (1875-1915), art dealer and collector, bequeathed 39 pictures from his modern collection to the National Gallery of Ireland. His intention was, however, contained in an unsigned codicil to his will and the matter was to cause bitter litigation between the British and Irish Governments because the National Gallery, London, claimed the pictures.

83 SPO S 14856A; 6 Sept. 1950.

84 TCD MS 8133(20); Beatty to McGreevy, 18 Nov. 1954.

85 TCD MS 8133(21); 1 Dec. 1954.

86 For an excellent synopsis of the Lane pictures controversy, see *The City's Art – the Original Municipal Collection* (Exhibition Catalogue, Dublin 1984), intro. by James White.

87 TCD MS 8133(32); Beatty to McGreevy, 31 Jan. 1956.

88 *Illustrated Summary Catalogue of the Paintings* (Dublin, 1981), pp 351-2.

89 *Illustrated Summary Catalogue of Drawings, Watercolours and Miniatures* (Dublin, 1983), pp 817-9.

90 *Catalogue of the Sculptures* (Dublin, 1975).

91 NGI CB 1952-5; 6 Jan. 1954.

92 TCD MS 8133(6); 5 Dec. 1952.

93 NGI CB 1952-5; 6 Jan. 1954.

94 The collection was the finest of its kind ever exhibited in Dublin. There were paintings by, amongst others: Manet, Monet, Renoir, Pissarro, Sisley, Degas, Van Gogh, Vuillard, Cézanne, Redon, Dérain and Dufy. Beatty's preference in oil painting was for landscapes. He admired some Impressionist painters but thought the prices paid for their works by American collectors to be proof of the folly of the art market. He had no sympathy for modern art (see *The Times*, 8 Feb. 1965). For a more detailed account of this affair, see Brian P. Kennedy, 'Alfred Chester Beatty and the National Gallery of Ireland', *Irish Arts Review*, Vol. 4, No. 1, Spring 1987, pp 41-54.

95 NGI CB 1952-5; 13 Sept. 1954.

96 *Ibid.*, Sept. 1954.

97 NGI CB 1956-8; note in McGreevy's handwriting, 10 May 1957.

98 NGI CB 1959; 22 June 1959.

99 NGI CB 1960-6; 12 Apr. 1962. There were three paintings still unpurchased: a Degas (£60,000), a Van Gogh (£40,000), and a Seurat (£12,000).
100 *Ibid.*, 16 Apr. 1962.
101 *Ibid.*, 21 Sept. 1962.
102 CBP; 20 Jan. 1955.
103 *Exhibition of Japanese Prints from the Collection of Sir Chester Beatty* (Dublin, 1955). There were 132 prints by 26 artists on display.
104 *Irish Times*, 11 May, 1955.
105 *Western Illuminated Manuscripts from the Library of Sir Chester Beatty* (Dublin, 1955). There were 34 manuscripts on exhibition, six of which had previously been on loan to the British Museum.
106 CBP; Beatty to Wilkinson, 14 Jan. 1954.
107 *Ibid.*, 22 Dec. 1953.
108 CBP; Beatty to R.J. Hayes, 16 Dec. 1961.
109 CBP; 26 Mar. 1955.
110 A sample list of experts whom Beatty invited to Dublin reveals a formidable array of talent — William Watson, Robert Skelton, Jack Hillier, Basil Gray, T.C. Skeat, Basil Robinson, I.E.S. Edwards, Arthur Arberry, Henry McAleavy, R. Soame Jenyns, D.S. Rice, Richard Ettinghausen, and S. Cary Welch.
111 CBP; 17 Jan. 1955.
112 CBP; Beatty to Wilkinson, 24 Jan. 1955.
113 CBP; McGillicuddy to Wilkinson, 31 Jan. 1955.
114 CBP; Revenue Commissioners to Wilkinson, 1 May 1956.
115 CBP; 3 May 1956.
116 Joan O'Neill told the author (23 Feb. 1984) that whenever she wrote or telephoned a government department on Beatty's behalf, she always received immediate attention.
117 E.g. SPO S 14856C; telegram from Costello to Beatty, 7 Feb. 1955.
118 City Hall Archive; Minute Book, 7 Nov. 1955. The resolution was moved by the Lord Mayor, Councillor Denis Larkin, T.D., and seconded by Councillor Robert Briscoe, T.D., P.C. The assistance of Ms Mary Clark is gratefully acknowledged.
119 CBP; 11 Nov. 1955.
120 It is customary for flags in Dublin to be flown at half-mast on the death of a Freeman.
121 City Hall Archive; Minute Book, 26 July 1956.
122 *Irish Independent*, 27 July 1956.
123 *Ibid.*, See above, p. 72.
124 *Irish Times*, 8 Aug. 1957.
125 D/Ex A 361/121; F.C. Connolly (Asst. Secretary, Dept. of Justice) to Seán Murphy (Secretary, Dept. of External Affairs), 31 Dec. 1956, and Murphy's reply, 5 Jan. 1957. Both letters are marked 'Strictly Confidential'.
126 Prior to the 1956 Act, the relevant law was contained in the Irish

Nationality and Citizenship Acts, 1935 and 1937. Section 5 of the 1935 Act empowered the Government to award a certificate of naturalisation to persons who had done signal honour or rendered distinguished service to the Irish nation. The provision had been used regarding three people, Mrs Mary Alden Childers and her sons, Erskine and Robert (issued 1938).

127 SPO S 16156; 9 Jan. 1957.

128 *Ibid.*, 11 Jan. 1957.

129 *Ibid.*, 15 Jan. 1957.

130 *Iris Oifigiúil*, 25 Jan. 1957.

131 *Irish Press*, 10 Aug. 1957.

132 *Irish Times*, 8 Aug. 1957.

133 SPO S 15345B. The speech was widely reported in the newspapers. *Sunday Press*, 24 Aug. 1957, *Irish Independent*, 25 and 26 Aug. 1957, *Irish Press* and *Irish Times*, 26 Aug. 1957.

134 Among the many distinguished visitors to the Chester Beatty Library were: Prince Pierre of Monaco, Cardinal Agagianian (the Papal Legate), Field Marshal Ayub Khan (President of Pakistan), and ex-King Umberto of Italy.

135 D/Ex A 361/121.

136 *Ibid.* Diplomatic passport No. D.13/60 was issued by the Passport Office on 22 June 1960, and renewed in 1965 until 22 June 1970.

137 CBP; British passport No. 1696069, issued 9 Aug. 1950. Beatty was not permitted to spend more than six months of each year in France. He purchased houses in Monte Carlo and at Lisbon and kept a permanent suite at the Grosvenor Hotel in London. By spending short periods in each of these cities and living in Dublin from May to September, Beatty avoided problems with the French authorities.

138 CBP; 26 Jan. 1959. The particular and paternal blessing of the Sovereign Pontiff noted Sir Chester's work 'in the field of Scripture studies' and his 'encouragement of humanitarian and charitable enterprises'.

139 *Dublin Evening Mail*, 19 June 1961. Cardinal Agagianian was most impressed by the Chester Beatty Library. He told Beatty: 'Dublin will be very grateful and will remember you for many centuries'.

140 D/Ex A 436/191; 16 Mar. 1964.

141 *Ibid.*, Apr. 1964.

142 Vatican Archive, Cummins to Mgr Nasalli Rocca, 15 & 25 Apr. 1964. The author is grateful to Don Pasquale Macchi for locating these letters.

143 TCD MS 8133(94); 18 May 1964.

144 *Irish Press*, 8 July 1960.

145 *Sunday Independent*, 22 Oct. 1957.

146 *Sunday Press*, 22 Sept. 1963.

147 *The Times*, 8 Feb. 1965.

148 For a short story based on Beatty's personality, see Terence de Vere White, *Big Fleas and LittleFleas* (London, 1976), pp 40-52. Beatty said the reason why he got asthma and rheumatism was because: 'As Mark Twain said: "Fleas are given to a dog to let him know he is alive".' (TCD MS 8133(29); Beatty to McGreevy, 22 Nov. 1955).

149 Beatty had a valet from the 1940s onwards, an Englishman called Frazer, until 1958, and then a Frenchman called Jacques. Among the luxuries which his valet provided, Beatty enjoyed having his newspaper ironed in the morning to remove any creases.

150 Bence-Jones, *Burke's Guide to Country Houses*, Vol. I, Ireland, pp 248-9.

151 CBP; Beatty to Hayes, 16 Jan. 1958.

152 Seán T. O'Kelly was 76 on 25 Aug. 1958. During the former President's last illness, Beatty arranged, at his own expense, to have a Harley Street cancer specialist flown over from London. The disease was too far advanced and, to Beatty's sorrow, his friend died on 23 Nov. 1966.

153 CBP; Beatty to General Eisenhower, 9 Mar. 1951.

154 *Evening Herald*, 11 July 1950.

155 CBP; Beatty to General Eisenhower, 9 Mar. 1951.

156 *The Times*, 22 Jan. 1968.

157 UCD A; McGilligan Papers, Beatty to McGilligan, 6 Sept. 1955, with attached report by H.J. Hinves titled 'The Taxation of Individuals in the Republic of Ireland', 19 July 1955. The author is grateful to Mr John McGilligan for drawing his attention to these papers.

158 *Ibid.*

159 *Ibid.*

160 See above, Chapter 3, p. 50. In 1955/56, the British standard rate of income tax was 8s. 6d. and surtax 10s. 0d; the comparative Irish rates were 7s. 6d. and 8s. 6d.

161 UCD A; McGilligan Papers, Hinves's report, Appendices A to E.

162 *Sunday Review*, 2 Sept. 1962.

163 Sheila Wingfield, *Sun Too Fast*, p. 224.

164 *Dáil Debates*, 149, 423-4, 10 Mar. 1955.

165 *Ibid.*, 234, 1202, 9 May 1968.

166 Interview with Jack Lynch, 1, Feb. 1985.

167 Interview with Evanna McGilligan, 14 Mar. 1984.

168 Bence-Jones, *Burke's Guide to Country Houses*, Vol. I, Ireland, p. 87.

169 *Sunday Dispatch*, 16 Aug. 1958. See also *Irish Independent*, 22 Feb. and 2 Aug. 1957.

170 CBP; Evanna McGilligan to John Wooderson, 25 Oct. 1957.

171 CBP; R.J. Hayes to Beatty, 31 Oct. 1958.

172 Interview with Joan O'Neill, 23 Feb. 1984.

173 Wireless for the Blind Fund, 10 Lower Hatch Street, Dublin; Chester Beatty files. Between 1952 and 1968 Beatty donated a

total of £21,023. The author is grateful to Ms Patricia McLoughlin for her assistance.

174 *Ibid.*, the appeals were broadcast on 3 July 1955 and 25 Dec. 1956.

175 TCD MS 8133(81); 10 Nov. 1961.

176 Interview with Joan O'Neill, 3 Apr. 1984. Beatty left a tenth of his residuary estate to be used for charitable purposes. His executors chose to make a gift to the Meath Hospital and it was used to equip a special 'Chester Beatty Unit'.

NOTES TO CHAPTER 5 (pp 108-148)

1 CBP; Beatty to Dr Bodmer, 20 Nov. 1963.

2 See above, Chapter 3, pp 54-5.

3 CBP; 8 Nov. 1953. This library in Beatty's native city had been established as a public institution by J.P. Morgan (1867-1943) in memory of his father, Pierpont Morgan (1837-1913), the founder.

4 *Irish Independent*, 12 Aug. 1954. The newspaper article quoted Beatty as saying: 'I have always wanted to found a library in Dublin more or less on the lines of the great Morgan Library in New York'.

5 Pierpont Morgan Library Archive; Indenture of Trust, 15 Feb. 1924, Section 3(1). The assistance of Mr Frederick C. Schroeder is gratefully acknowledged.

6 *Ibid.*, J.P. Morgan to the Trustees, 15 Feb. 1924.

7 *Irish Tatler and Sketch*, May 1956.

8 CBP, Beatty to Wilkinson, 5 May 1956.

9 CBP; Beatty to Wilkinson, second letter, 5 May 1956.

10 *The Times*, 31 Jan. 1957, unsigned obituary.

11 *Irish Times*, 23 Jan. 1976, obituary by Alf MacLochlainn. Richard James Hayes was born at Abbeyfeale, County Limerick, in 1902. His academic prowess was signalled by his being in the first three places nationally in each of six subjects in the Intermediate and Leaving Certificate examinations. At Trinity he won medals for mathematics and had the unique distinction of taking three Honours degrees simultaneously — in Celtic Studies, Modern Languages and Philosophy. He later completed a doctorate in law. He was appointed Director of the National Library at the age of 38.

12 It is said that Hayes, an ardent nationalist, deliberately stipulated that he should be cremated so that his friends and relatives would have to make the journey across the border into Northern Ireland. There was no crematorium in the Republic of Ireland at the time.

13 CBP; Beatty to Hayes, 1 Apr. 1957.

14 SPO S 15345B; the letter is undated but it must have been written in late April because de Valera replied on 6 May: 'I have just received your letter'.

15 *Ibid.*

16 *Ibid.*, 6 May 1957.

17 NGI CB 1959, Beatty to McGreevy, 17 Mar. 1959.

18 SPO S 15345B; Hayes to Moynihan, 27 June 1959.

19 *Ibid*; Hayes to Moynihan, 9 Aug. 1957.

20 *Ibid.*, 19 Aug. 1957.

21 *Irish Times*, 26 Aug. 1957.

22 *Irish Independent*, 3 Nov. 1957, unsigned obituary.

23 Beatty often addressed his letters to Hayes: 'My dear "Bombe Atomique" '.

24 By the time of Beatty's death in 1968, Hayes had already supervised the publication of 57 catalogues.

25 CBP; Beatty to Hayes, 19 Mar. 1958.

26 *Ibid.*, 25 Apr. 1958.

27 *Ibid.*, 29 Dec. 1958. Samuel Pepys left his library as a gift to Magdalene College, Cambridge, with the proviso that should Magdalene fail to carry out his wishes, the library would fall to Trinity College, Cambridge.

28 See above, Chapter 2, p. 21.

29 CBP; 6 Feb. 1959.

30 CBP; 17 Feb. 1959.

31 CBP; undated notes by Hayes titled 'Comments on draft codicil'.

32 *Irish Times*, 27 Jan. 1981.

33 NGI CB 1951; 1 Dec. 1951.

34 TCD MS 8133(9); 11 Feb. 1953.

35 CBP; builders' contracts: original library − £21,572; librarian's house − £4,583; library extension − £17,592. These figures do not include the cost of furnishings. The purchase price of 10 Ailesbury Road and of Clonmannon Estate is not known.

36 Beatty bought material for most of his major art collections and created a number of minor collections during the 1950s. Between 1953 and 1960, Beatty spent £3,600 on Japanese prints alone (CBP; Beatty to Evanna McGilligan, 16 Apr. 1960).

37 The cost of maintaining the library for the year ended 31 Aug. 1967 was £5,253 (CBP; Wooderson to Hayes, 2 Jan. 1968).

38 E.g. In 1959 Beatty financed an extension to the Royal Cancer Hospital in London. It is known today as The Chester Beatty Research Institute of the Institute for Cancer Research. (See above, Chapter 2, p. 36).

39 CBP; 23 Apr. 1959. The original amount of Morgan's endowment fund was $1.5 million.

40 *Ibid.*

41 R.J. Hayes, *The Chester Beatty Library, Dublin* (Dublin, 1958), p. 5.

42 CBP; Beatty to Hayes, 25 Feb. 1959.

43 *Ibid.*

44 Bill Allen met Beatty at the dinner following the opening of the Chester Beatty Collection at the National Gallery of Ireland, 6

Sept. 1950. Author, soldier, traveller, businessman and farmer, Allen had lived an adventurous life which would have appealed to Beatty. See *Irish Times*, 1 Oct. 1973, obituary by Seán MacEntee.

45 CBP; 14 Apr. 1959.

46 *Ibid.*

47 CBP; 23 Apr. 1959.

48 SPO S 15345B; note by Moynihan, 22 Dec. 1959.

49 *Ibid.*, 3 Feb. 1960.

50 The papers had been left by Máirtín Ó Flathartaigh, Assistant Secretary, Dept. of Education, on his transfer to the post of Secretary to the President.

51 SPO S 15345B; note by Nolan, 25 Oct. 1960.

52 CBP; Hayes to McGillicuddy, 6 Nov. 1960.

53 *Ibid.*

54 *Ibid.*

55 CBP; Hayes to Beatty, 8 Nov. 1960.

56 SPO S 15345B; 3 Dec. 1960.

57 *Ibid.*, Nolan to Darley & Co., 17 Jan. 1961.

58 *Ibid.*, note by Lemass, 6 Dec. 1960.

59 CBP; 10 Jan. 1961.

60 SPO S 15345B; 17 Jan. 1961.

61 *Ibid*; Nolan to Darley & Co., 19 Jan. 1961.

62 Finance Act, 1961, Part III (Death Duties), Section 23(1)(a).

63 *Ibid.*, Section 23(2).

64 CBP; 21 Apr. 1961.

65 See above, Chapter 4, pp 65-6.

66 CBP; 16 Oct. 1961. The site was at the junction of Northumberland Road and Haddington Road.

67 CBP; McGillicuddy to Beatty, 20 Aug. 1962.

68 CBP; Beatty to McGillicuddy, 4 Sept. 1962.

69 *Ibid.*

70 The sale took place on 3 Dec. 1962. See *Irish Times*, 4 Dec. 1962. The second part of the sale in June 1963 raised £100,558.

71 SPO S 15345B; 3 Oct. 1963.

72 *Ibid.*, The Royal Dublin Society Showgrounds bordered the rear of the Chester Beatty Library.

73 *Ibid.*; 4 Oct. 1963.

74 *Ibid.*, 5 Oct. 1963.

75 *Ibid.*, 7 Oct. 1963.

76 *Ibid.*, memorandum by Ó Cearbhaill, 9 Oct. 1963. It was noted that the Taoiseach wished to be informed of any developments in the matter.

77 CBP; 17 Oct. 1963. See above, Chapter 3, p. 49.

78 For a description of the Bodmer Library at Cologny, Geneva, see *The Book Collector*, Vol. 7, pp 381-95, and Vol. 8, pp 31-45 (London, 1958 & 1959).

79 CBP; 17 Oct. 1963.

80 CBP; 20 Nov. 1963. Beatty's comments recall his letter to the

Archbishop of Canterbury regarding Sir John Forsdyke. See above, Chapter 3, p. 61.

81 Bodmer bequeathed his library to a private foundation. Subsidised by the Canton of Geneva, the Bibliotheca Bodmeriana was opened to the public on 15 June 1972.

82 SPO S 15345B; 12 Aug. 1964.

83 *Ibid.*; 13 Aug. 1964.

84 Succession Act, 1965; Section 117(1) & (2).

85 *Irish Times*, 8 Feb. 1965. The British Academy also congratulated Beatty by presenting him with an Address of Honour to offer 'its profound gratitude' and 'affectionate good wishes' to 'an outstanding Patron of Learning' (see *The Times*, 8 Feb. 1965).

86 Beatty had revised the list of Trustees in his Will. They were now R.J. Hayes (Chairman), Cearbhall Ó Dálaigh, C.S. Andrews and Terence de Vere White.

87 CBP; 28 July 1965.

88 CBP; Lemass to Hayes, 5 Aug. 1965.

89 SPO S 15345B; 5 Aug. 1965.

90 *Ibid.*, 10 Aug. 1965.

91 *Ibid*; 12 Aug. 1965.

92 SPO CAB G.C. 11/20 Item 5; 17 Aug. 1965.

93 SPO S 15345B; Lemass to the Trustees, 17 Aug. 1965.

94 CBP; 23 Aug. 1965.

95 CBP; Hayes to Terence de Vere White, undated.

96 CBP; undated.

97 *Irish Independent*, 8 Nov. 1965. See also *Sunday Express*, 7 Nov. 1965.

98 SPO S 15345B; Lemass to Jack Lynch, 17 Aug. 1965.

99 CBP; 16 Nov. 1965.

100 SPO S 15345B; series of letters – H. Mundow (O.P.W.) to M. Breathnach (Asst. Sec., Dept. of Finance), 21 Dec. 1965; Breathnach to Dr N.G. Nolan, 7 Jan. 1966; Nolan to Breathnach, 7 Jan. 1966 B. Fanning (O.P.W.) to Hayes, 3 June, 1966; Hayes to Fanning, 8 June 1966.

101 *Evening Press*, 17 Aug. 1966, and *Irish Press*, 18 Aug. 1966. The de Valeras were accompanied by two of their grandchildren, Ann and Eamon.

102 CBP; undated notes written by Hayes regarding Beatty's Will, p. 1.

103 *Ibid.*, p. 2.

104 *Ibid.*

105 *Ibid.*

106 *Ibid.*, p. 3.

107 Beatty's Will, 19 Aug. 1966, Section V, Clause (6), Paragraph (4).

108 *Ibid.*, Section V(1).

109 CBP; undated notes by Hayes.

110 Will, V(4)(i).

111 *Ibid.*, V(4)(f).

112 *Ibid.*, VIII(3), (a) to (q).

113 *Ibid.*, VI & VII. Beatty's Will did not specify the amounts involved. The two Trust Funds were called the Chester Beatty Library Trust and the Clonmannon Trust.
114 Interview with Dr David James, 6 Apr. 1984. After Beatty's death, Hayes often used this phrase to refer to the Chester Beatty Library.
115 CBP; notes prepared for Beatty by Hayes, undated but clearly written in 1966.
116 In Sept. 1951 Beatty received 'a special notice of deepest appreciation' from the President and Trustees of Columbia University on behalf of the faculty of Engineering. The notice acknowledged Beatty's support in making 'a reality of Columbia's vision of a great engineering center'. In July 1954 the President of Columbia University (General Eisenhower) sent Beatty a scroll of authorisation to represent the University at ceremonies in Dublin to celebrate the centenary of the Catholic University of Ireland.
117 *Princeton Packet,* 1 Mar. 1967.
118 Codicil to Will, 18 Aug. 1966.
119 CBP; 8 Nov. 1966.
120 CBP; 20 Nov. 1966.
121 *Selected Manuscripts from the Chester Beatty Library* (Princeton, New Jersey, 1967). Exhibition held from 28 Feb. to 13 May 1967.
122 *New York Times,* 28 Feb. 1967.
123 CBP; Hayes to Beatty, 10 Mar. 1967.
124 CBP; Fitzgerald to Beatty, 8 Mar. 1967.
125 *Ibid.*
126 *Ibid.*
127 CBP; Fitzgerald to Hayes, 16 Mar. 1967.
128 CBP; 16 Mar. 1967.
129 CBP; 31 Mar. 1967.
130 Beatty to Evanna McGilligan, 16 May, 1967. Letter in Ms McGilligan's possession.
131 CBP; 26 Apr. 1967.
132 CBP; 14 June 1967.
133 The paintings had been withdrawn from the Chester Beatty Library bequest in a codicil of 20 Apr. 1967. No records were made at the sale but the prices were good, the highest being £42,000 for a painting by Picasso. See *Evening Press,* 28 June 1967; *Irish Times* and *The Times,* 29 June 1967.
134 CBP; 15 Dec. 1964.
135 CBP; Kraus to Croasdella Cruess Callaghan, 16 Nov. 1957.
136 CBP; Callaghan to Kraus, 23 Dec. 1957.
137 See Kraus, *A Rare Book Saga,* pp 209-10.
138 *Ibid.*, chap. 28, pp. 205-10.
139 *Ibid.*, p. 207.
140 A Thebaid of Statius and a Psalter of Philip II.
141 *A Rare Book Saga,* p. 208.
142 *Ibid.*

143 CBP; the letter is reproduced in *A Rare Book Saga*, pp 208-9.
144 CBP; 30 June 1967.
145 CBP; 4 July 1967.
146 *Ibid*. The nature of Beatty's friendship with the Comtesse d'Aubigny d'Esymards is not known, but they were acquainted for at least 20 years. Beatty sent the Comtesse copies of his published catalogues during the 1940s. There are frequent references to her in the McGreevy papers and these indicate that Beatty saw her regularly while he was in France.
147 *Ibid*.
148 CBP; 8 July 1967.
149 Five people in fact — Beatty, Hayes, Bruhl, Hosking and Fitzgerald.
150 CBP; 5 July 1967.
151 CBP; 13 July 1967.
152 *Ibid.*
153 CBP; 17 July 1967.
154 The publication had been a monumental task involving sources assembled from 678 libraries in 30 countries and from over 600 private collections. In recognition of his work, Hayes also received honorary degrees from the National University of Ireland and from Queen's University, Belfast.
155 CBP; 12 July 1967.
156 CBP; 24 July 1967.
157 CBP; 1 Aug. 1967.
158 CBP; 5 Aug. 1967.
159 *Sunday Press*, 13 Aug. 1967. Article headlined 'Retiring to devote time to Library'.
160 CBP; Hayes to Fitzgerald, 19 Aug. 1967. Notes enclosed with letter.
161 *Ibid.*
162 Interview with Terence de Vere White, 30 May 1984.
163 CBP; 28 Aug. 1967.
164 CBP; 2 Oct. 1967.
165 CBP; 27 Oct. 1967. The Chester Beatty Western Manuscripts were sold at Sotheby's in two parts. The first sale took place on 3 Dec. 1968 (world record sale total £363,850), the second on 24 June 1969 (sale total £391,750). Kraus bought four manuscripts at the second sale (total paid £128,500).
166 CBP; Hayes to Beatty, 31 Oct. 1967, and Bruhl to Hayes, 15 Nov. 1967.
167 CBP; 3 Dec. 1967.
168 CBP; 12 Dec. 1967.

NOTES TO CHAPTER 6 (pp 149-158)

1 The Little Sisters of the Assumption, the Little Sisters of the Poor,

the Irish Sisters of Charity and the Anglican Sisters. Beatty had always given alms generously at his door and had supported some of the local religious communities.

2 *Irish Times*, 30 Jan. 1968.

3 At the State Funeral of President Douglas Hyde in 1949, President O'Kelly and the Taoiseach, Mr de Valera, had remained outside St Patrick's Cathedral during the service.

4 *Irish Press*, 6 Feb. 1968.

5 *The Pallotine*, Sept. 1968.

6 *Irish Independent*, 22 Jan. 1968.

7 *Ibid.*

8 *Irish Times* and *Irish Press*, 22 Jan. 1968; *Cork Examiner* 23 Jan. 1968; *Irish Independent*, 29 Jan. 1968.

9 Headline of the obituary in *The Times*, 22 Jan. 1968. See also *Daily Telegraph*, 22 Jan. 1968.

10 SPO S 15345B; Kevin Mangan, Attorney General's Office, to Dr N.G. Nolan, 19 Mar. 1968.

11 *Seanad Debates*, 64, 1234-35, 8 May 1968, and *Dáil Debates*, 234, 1201-05, 9 May 1968.

12 A State grant-in-aid to the Chester Beatty Library began in 1969 at a sum of £12,000.

13 CBP. The speech was reported in the *Irish Times*, 28 July 1975.

14 De Valera's treatment of Beatty supports Professor Donal McCartney's view that: 'As long as Irish history is discussed, there will be controversy over de Valera's political, social and economic achievements and failures. It will be remembered to his credit, however, that he set aside pennies from a poor state and an impoverished people for the cultivation of things of the mind, and that he gave generously of his own time to help the advancement of higher learning'. *The National University of Ireland and Eamon de Valera* (Dublin, 1983).

Appendix A
Beatty's Irish Ancestry
(1875-1968)

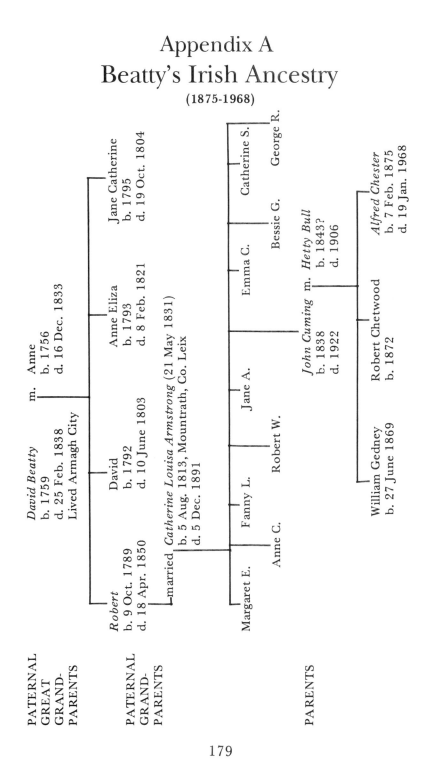

PATERNAL GREAT GRAND-PARENTS

PATERNAL GRAND-PARENTS

PARENTS

Appendix B

Chronology

1875 February 7	Birth of A. Chester Beatty in New York.
1898 June 8	Qualifies with a degree of Engineer of Mines from Columbia University, New York, and travels west to Denver, Colorado, where he begins his career shovelling rock in a mine.
1900 April 18	Marries Grace Madeleine Rickard. Two children, Ninette (born 1901) and Alfred Chester (born 1907).
1903-08	Works as Assistant Chief Engineer with the Guggenheim Exploration Company.
1911 March 28	Death of his wife from typhoid fever. His own health was impaired, suffering from silicosis.
1913 June 21	Marries Edith Dunn and they settle in London.
1914 December 22	Registers a new mining company in London called Selection Trust.
Winter	Visits Egypt.
1917	Almost fatal illness. Doctors advise a world health cruise. Travels to Japan and China.

1920s	Selection Trust Limited becomes a group of companies with interests in many countries, including Russia, Serbia, Gold Coast and Northern Rhodesia.
1933	Becomes a naturalised British Citizen.
1939-45	Committed to the Allied war effort, he serves on a number of British Government-appointed committees.
1950 May	Moves to Dublin where he had bought a house at 10 Ailesbury Road.
July	Presents gift of 93 paintings to the Irish Nation (mainly French 19th century works of the Barbizon School).
1952	Death of his second wife, Edith.
1953 September 24	Presents gift of 143 items of rare Oriental weaponry to the Irish Nation.
1954 July 6	Knighthood conferred on Alfred Chester Beatty by Queen Elizabeth II at Buckingham Palace, London.
August 11	The Chester Beatty Library, 20 Shrewsbury Road, Dublin, is officially opened to the public.
1957 January 19	Becomes the first Honorary Irish Citizen.
August 24	Formal opening of a new exhibition gallery at the Chester Beatty Library.
1968 January 19	Death of Alfred Chester Beatty at the Princess Grace Clinic, Monte Carlo, Monaco, in his 93rd year.

Notes on Sources and Bibliography

Synopsis

1. **NOTE ON SOURCES**
2. **PRIMARY SOURCES:**
    - (a) Manuscript material.
    - (b) Printed material:
        - I. Newspapers and other periodicals
        - II. Official publications
        - III. Catalogues
        - IV. Annual reports.
    - (c) Interviews.
3. **SECONDARY SOURCES:**
    - (a) Biographical and reference works.
    - (b) Unpublished theses.
    - (c) Books.
    - (d) Articles.

1. NOTE ON SOURCES

There are particular problems to be encountered in attempting to research near-contemporary history. Arguably, a near-contemporary topic offers less scope for objectivity. But it also offers important possibilities such as the opportunity to interview people who participated closely in the events being researched.

It is evident that one must rely heavily on written sources.

Here again, the historian of a near-contemporary topic encounters obstacles. It is often difficult to gain access to relevant papers held by government departments. Many correspondents are still alive and are hesitant to allow their letters to be subjected to close scrutiny.

The case history of Alfred Chester Beatty and Ireland is without doubt a positive research topic. But, as a study in cultural politics, it was essential that Beatty's correspondence and that of politicians and civil servants be made available. Fortunately, these papers were released and it is pleasing to acknowledge the co-operation of the authorities involved.

The Chester Beatty Papers (Chester Beatty Library, Dublin) provided the most important source of material. Beatty was an inveterate letter-writer. Since he lived in Dublin for only four months of each year, he kept in touch with his librarian by letter. He also made considerable use of the telephone. This does not pose much of a problem, however, because he tended to confirm anything he said on the telephone by letter, and copies were always retained. Many of Beatty's letters can be consulted in both his personal papers and in government department files.

The Chester Beatty files in the Department of the Taoiseach and in the Department of Foreign Affairs were useful in documenting the Government's official policy of encouraging Chester Beatty. There was no evidence that papers had been removed from the files before they were made available by the State Paper Office and the Public Record Office.

The papers of Thomas McGreevy (National Gallery of Ireland and Trinity College) were more important than had been anticipated. His friendship with Beatty enabled him to discuss personal matters which are not disclosed elsewhere.

Beatty's business correspondence (London School of Economics) contains some relevant material, for example, his retirement speech, but there is little of his correspondence after he moved to Dublin. Other important though limited material was consulted at archives in Dublin (City Hall; Shelbourne Hotel; University College, Dublin, Archive Department (Stephen's Green); Wireless for the Blind Fund (Hatch Street)); London (British Museum; Victoria and Albert Museum), Rome (Vatican Library); New York (Columbia

University; Pierpont Morgan Library); and New Jersey (Princeton University).

A most important source of material was the coverage of Beatty's affairs by British and Irish newspapers. It was possible to cross-check much of the information by consulting a number of newspapers for any given day.

The debates of the House of Commons, Westminster, were used to gauge the rising Conservative Party dissatisfaction with the policies of the Labour Party Government. The Irish Dáil and Seanad debates record the level of political awareness of Beatty's activities in Ireland.

Other useful primary material was found in art exhibition and sale catalogues, and in the annual reports of Beatty's mining company, Selection Trust Limited.

Recorded interviews and correspondence with Beatty's friends, acquaintances and staff provided important information which allowed a fuller understanding of his activities in Ireland. While such interviews were only of supplementary value to the written sources, they often pointed the way to interesting lines of enquiry.

The length and scope of Beatty's career involved the use of a wide range of secondary sources. The most relevant of these should have been Arthur Wilson's biography of Beatty. This is an enjoyable book which repeats many familiar but unverified stories. It is similar in tone to the unpublished biography of Beatty by John Murdoch and many of the statements are repeated. It is not intended to be a scholarly work and is of limited use in the preparation of an academic study.

While articles and pamphlets sometimes provided interesting details, they tended to repeat inaccuracies regarding dates. As in the case of newspapers, they required cautious and dispassionate treatment.

2. PRIMARY SOURCES

(a) *Manuscript material.*

Chester Beatty Library, Dublin	— Unpublished memoirs of Alfred Chester Beatty, 3 Vols. — Beatty correspondence, 30 box files. — Typescripts of interviews given by Beatty to a Dublin journalist, John Murdoch, who was commissioned in 1958 to write Beatty's biography. The book was never published but three draft volumes survive. — Memorabilia of Alfred Chester Beatty. — Newspaper cuttings.
British Museum, London	— Standing Committee Minute Books, 1923-63. — Board of Trustees Minute Books, 1963-8.
Columbia University, New York; Library Archive	— Examination Record Books.
Dublin City Hall	— Municipal Council of the City of Dublin, Minute Books.
London School of Economics, British Library of Political and Economic Science	— Business correspondence of Alfred Chester Beatty. i) Historical files, 150 boxes. ii) ACB series, 56 boxes.
National Gallery of Ireland; Library Archive	— Chester Beatty files, 1951-77.
National Library of Ireland	— Newspaper files.
Pierpont Morgan Library, New York; Library Archive	— Letters of J.P. Morgan regarding the foundation of the Library.

Princeton University, New — Records of the Class of 1897.
Jersey; Library Archive

Public Record Office, — Chester Beatty files of the
Dublin Department of External Affairs.

338/316 Mr Chester Beatty. Presentation of Pictures to the National Gallery.

338/660 The Chester Beatty Library, Dublin.

339/49/48 Funeral of Sir Chester Beatty.

342/2258 Authentication of Certificate of Nationality of Sir Chester Beatty. Darley & Co., Solicitors, Kildare Street.

361/121 Conferring of Irish Citizenship on Sir Chester Beatty as a token of honour. Also visit to Portugal, 1962.

436/191 Sir A. Chester Beatty. Visit to Rome, April 1964.

Shelbourne Hotel, Dublin — Hotel Registers, 1937-68.

State Paper Office, Dublin — Chester Beatty files of the Department of the Taoiseach 1949-68.

S 14856 A & B and Annexes A & B. Presentation of Chester Beatty Paintings to the Nation. (Annexes refer to the exhibition catalogue, July 1950).

S 14856 C Alfred Chester Beatty, Presentation to the Nation of Collection of Paintings.

S 15345 A & B Sir Alfred Chester Beatty. Collection of Oriental

Manuscripts and Weapons.

S 15749   Sir Alfred Chester Beatty. Portrait by Seán O'Sullivan commissioned by An Chomhairle Ealaíon.

S 16156   Sir Alfred Chester Beatty. Grant of Irish Citizenship as token of honour, 1957.

S 18192   Sir Alfred Chester Beatty. Official Funeral.

S.P.O. Dublin

— Arts Council files of the Department of the Taoiseach.

S 14559   An Chomhairle Ealaíon.

S 14922   An Chomhairle Ealaíon.

S 15073 A   Appointment of Director and Ordinary Members of the Arts Council.

S 15226 A/I   Annual Reports and Accounts.

S 15424 Arts Act 1951 (Additional Function) re Order 1953 for Acquisition of Rotunda Buildings.

— S 15297 A An Tóstal. National Festival, 1953.

Trinity College, Dublin; Manuscript Room

— Correspondence of Thomas McGreevy
I) MS 8133 Sir Chester Beatty (1-100);
II) MS 8147 Arts Council (1-15).

University College, Dublin; Archive Department

— McGilligan Papers.

— Ó Dálaigh Papers.

Vatican Library — Papers of Monsignor Mario Nasalli Rocca di Cornelliano.

Victoria and Albert Museum, London — Chester Beatty files, 1923-58.

Wireless for the Blind Fund, Hatch Street, Dublin — Chester Beatty files, 1952-68.

(b) *Printed material.*

I. Newspapers and Periodicals

Càpuchin Annual
Cork Examiner
Daily Express
Daily Mail
Daily Telegraph
Dublin Evening Mail
Evening Herald
Evening Press
Irish Independent
Irish Press
Irish Review and Annual
Irish Tatler and Sketch

Irish Times
Leader
New York Times
Princeton Packet
Social and Personal
Sunday Dispatch
Sunday Express
Sunday Independent
Sunday Press
Sunday Review
The Times

II. Official Publications

Census of Population (Irish Free State and Republic), 1946 & 1951.

Census of Population of Ireland 1946 and 1951: General Report. Dublin, 1958.

Dáil Éireann. Parliamentary Debates: Official Report. Dublin, 1922-

Hansard. Parliamentary Debates of the House of Commons. London, 1945-

Report on the Arts in Ireland. Thomas Bodkin. Dublin, 1949.

Report of the Commission on Emigration and Other Population Problems. Dublin, 1954.

Seanad Éireann. Parliamentary Debates: Official Report. Dublin, 1922-

III. Catalogues

Chester Beatty Library — Catalogues of the Collections. 80 Vols.

Exhibition Catalogues:

The Chester Beatty Collection. National Gallery of Ireland, Dublin, 1950.

The Chester Beatty Biblical Papyri. Trinity College, Dublin, 1950.

Guide to the Manuscripts exhibited in the Library of Trinity College, Dublin, on the occasion of An Tóstal 1953.

Exhibition of Early Bronze Crucifixes and Bronze Statuettes of the Renaissance. College of Surgeons, Dublin, 1954.

Exhibition of Irish Bookbindings. Trinity College, Dublin, 1954.

Western Illuminated Manuscripts from the Library of Sir Chester Beatty. Trinity College, Dublin, 1955.

Exhibition of Japanese Prints from the Collection of Sir Chester Beatty. Trinity College, Dublin, 1955.

Exhibition of Paintings from Irish Collections. Municipal Gallery, Dublin, 1957.

Persian Art from before and after the Mongol Conquest. Ann Arbor, Michigan, 1959.

Great Spanish Masters. National Museum, Stockholm, 1960.

Selected Manuscripts from the Chester Beatty Library. Princeton University Library, New Jersey, 1967.

Persian Miniature Paintings from Collections in the British Isles. Victoria and Albert Museum, London, 1967.

The City's Art — The Original Municipal Collection. Hugh Lane Municipal Gallery, Dublin, 1984.

National Gallery of Ireland Catalogues:

Catalogue of the Sculptures. Dublin, 1975.

Illustrated Summary Catalogue of Paintings. Dublin, 1981.

Illustrated Summary Catalogues of Drawings, Water Colours and Miniatures. Dublin, 1983.

Sale Catalogues:

Sale of Contents of 10 Ailesbury Road, Ballsbridge, Dublin 4. James Adam & Sons, 14 May, 1968.
Sale of Contents of Clonmannon House, Ashford, County Wicklow. James Adam & Sons, 21 May, 1968.
Sale of Contents of 6 Ailesbury Grove, Ballsbridge, Dublin 4. (Estate of Philis O'Ceallaigh). Lisney & Son, 14 March, 1984.

Sotheby & Co., Art Dealers, London — Sale Catalogues.

IV. Annual Reports

Selection Trust Limited — Annual Reports, 1922-81.

(c) *Interviews*

De HAMEL, Dr Christopher. London, 23 May 1984.
DOHERTY, Patrick. Dublin, 22 Mar. 1984.
FURLONG, Dr George. London, 29 May 1984.
GALVIN, Sir John. Dublin, 23 & 25 Aug. and 3 Sept. 1984.
GIERAN, Jim. Dublin, 13 Feb. 1985.
GRAY, Basil. Telephone conversation. Oxford, 1 June 1984.
HENCHY, Dr Patrick. Dublin, 2 Feb. 1984.
HENEGHAN, Joan. Telephone conversation. Dublin, 5 Apr. 1984.
HICKEY, Kieran. Dublin, 20 Feb. 1984.
HILLIER, Jack and Mary. Redhill, Surrey, 25 May 1984.
JAMES, Dr David. Dublin, 6 Apr. 1984.
KIDD, Cyril. London, 1 June 1984, and 8 July 1985.
LYNCH, Jack. Dublin, 13 Feb. 1985.
McGILLIGAN, Evanna. Dublin, 14 & 23 Mar. 1984.
O'NEILL, Joan. Dublin, 23 Feb. and 3 Apr. 1984.
ROBINSON, Basil. London, 29 May 1984.
SKELTON, Robert. London, 24 May 1984.
WATSON, Professor William. London, 26 May 1984.

WHITE, Dr James. Dublin, 2 Mar. 1984.
WHITE, Terence de Vere. London, 30 May 1984.

3. Secondary Sources

(a) *Biographical and Reference Works*

BENCE-JONES, Mark. *Burke's Guide to Country Houses*, Vol. I: Ireland. London, 1978.

Biographical Dictionary of American Labor Leaders. Ed. Gary M. Fink. Westport, Connecticut, 1974.

BOYLAN, Henry. *A Dictionary of Irish Biography*. Dublin, 1978.

Burke's Genealogical and Heraldic History of the Peerage, Baronetage and Knightage. London, 1959.

Debrett's Peerage, Baronetage, Knightage & Companionage. Ed. P.W. Montague-Smith. Kingston-upon-Thames, Surrey, 1968.

Dictionary of National Biography: 1961-70. Eds. E.T. Williams and C.S. Nicholls. Oxford, 1981.

FITZ-SIMON, Christopher. *The Arts in Ireland: A Chronology*. Dublin, 1982.

FORD, P. & G. *Select List of Reports of Inquiries of the Irish Dáil and Senate, 1922-1972*. Dublin, 1974.

HICKEY, D.J. and DOHERTY, J.E. *A Dictionary of Ireland since 1800*. Dublin, 1980.

Mining International Yearbook. London, 1977.

Mining Manual and Mining Yearbook. Ed. Walter Skinner, London, 1911-.

PALMER, Alan. *The Penguin Dictionary of Twentieth-Century History, 1900-1982*. Harmondsworth, Middlesex, 1983.

Reader's Encyclopedia of the American West. Ed. Howard R. Lamar, New York, 1977.

Simon's Taxes. 3rd Edn. 9 Vols. London, 1976.

Who's Who. London, 1948.

Who's Who in Switzerland 1964/65. Geneva, 1964.

Who Was Who in America with World Notables. Vol. V, 1969-73. Chicago, 1973.

World Biography, 1948. New York, 1948.

(b) *Unpublished Theses*

O'CALLAGHAN, Margaret M. *Language and Religion: The Quest for Identity in the Irish Free State.* Master of Arts, University College, Dublin, 1981.

RASTALL, Benjamen. *The Labour History of Cripple Creek.* Doctor of Philosophy, University of Wisconsin, 1906.

(c) *Books*

ADAMS, Michael. *Censorship: The Irish Experience.* Alabama, 1968.

AKENSON, D.H. *A Mirror to Kathleen's Face: Education in Independent Ireland.* Montreal and London, 1975.

ALLEN, F.L. *The Great Pierpont Morgan.* New York, 1949.

BEHRMAN, S.N. *Duveen.* London, 1952.

BODKIN, Thomas. *Hugh Lane and his Pictures.* 3rd Edn. Dublin, 1956.

BOWEN, Elizabeth. *The Shelbourne.* London, 1951.

BROWN, Terence. *Ireland — A Social and Cultural History 1922-79.* London, 1981.

CABANNE, Pierre. *The Great Collectors.* London, 1964.

CAMPBELL, Patrick. *My Life and Easy Times.* London, 1967.

CAUGHEY, John W. *Gold is Cornerstone.* Berkeley, California, 1948.

CHANDOS, Lord. *Memoirs of Lord Chandos* (Oliver Lyttelton). London, 1962.

CHILDS, David. *Britain since 1945: A Political History.* London, 1979.

CHURCHILL, Winston. *The Second World War.* Vol. V. London, 1952.

COLLIER, Richard. *The City that Wouldn't Die.* London, 1959.

CONLIN, Joseph Robert. *Big Bill Haywood and the Radical Union Movement.* Syracuse, New York, 1969.

CONSTABLE, W.G. *Art Collecting in the U.S.A.: An Outline of History,* London, 1964.

COOKE, C.A. *The Life of Sir Richard Stafford Cripps.* London, 1957.

COOPER, Douglas. Ed. *Great Private Collections*, London, 1964.

COWELL, John. *Where They Lived in Dublin*. Dublin, 1980.

DOOLAN, Brian. *Principles of Irish Law*. Dublin, 1981.

FANNING, Ronan. *The Irish Department of Finance 1922-58*. Dublin, 1978.

———. *Independent Ireland*. Dublin, 1983.

FOOT, Michael. *Aneurin Bevan. A Biography*. 2 Vols. London, 1962 and 1973.

FOWLES, Edward. *Memories of Duveen Brothers*. London, 1976.

GREGORY, Theodore. *Ernest Oppenheimer and the Economic Development of Southern Africa*. London, 1962.

GROGAN, Vincent. *The Principles and Practices of Irish Income Tax*. 2nd Edn. Dublin, 1952.

HAMMOND, John Hays. *The Autobiography of John Hays Hammond*. 2 Vols. New York, 1935.

HARRINGTON, William and YOUNG, Peter. *The 1945 Revolution*. London, 1978.

HAYWOOD, William 'Big Bill'. *Bill Haywood's Book – The Autobiography of William D. Haywood*. New York, 1929.

HERRMANN, Frank. *The English as Collectors*. London, 1972.

———. *Sotheby's: Portrait of an Auction House*. London, 1980.

HEWINS, Ralph. *Mr Five Per Cent: The Biography of Calouste Gulbenkian*. London, 1957.

HOOVER, Herbert. *The Memoirs of Herbert Hoover. Years of Adventure, 1874-1920*. London, 1952.

HOPKINS, Harry. *The New Look. A Social History of the Forties and Fifties in Britain*, London, 1963.

INGLIS, Brian. *West Briton*. London, 1962.

KRAUS, H.P. *A Rare Book Saga*, London, 1979.

LOW, Sir David. *Low Visibility: A Cartoon History, 1945-53*. London, 1953.

———. *Autobiography*. London, 1956.

———. *The Fearful Fifties*. London, 1960.

LYONS, F.S.L. *Ireland since the Famine*. London, paperback edn., 1973.

———. *Culture and Anarchy in Ireland, 1890-1939*. Oxford, 1979.

LYSAGHT, Charles E. *Brendan Bracken*. London, 1979.

McHUGH, Robert. Ed. *Jack B. Yeats: A Centenary Gathering*. Dublin, 1971.

MACMILLAN, Harold. *The Blast of War 1939-45*. London, 1957.

MARKS, Richard. *Burrell: Portrait of a Collector*. Glasgow, 1983.

MEENAN, James. *The Irish Economy since 1922*. Liverpool, 1970.

MILLER, Edward. *That Noble Cabinet. A History of the British Museum*. London, 1973.

MOYNIHAN, Maurice. *Currency and Central Banking in Ireland, 1922-1960*. Dublin, 1975.

———. Ed. *Speeches and Statements by Eamon de Valera 1917-73*. Dublin, 1980.

MUNBY, A.N.L. *The Dispersal of the Phillips Library*. 5 Vols. Cambridge, 1951-60.

MURPHY, John A. *Ireland in the Twentieth Century*. Dublin, 1975.

NASH, George H. *The Life of Herbert Hoover. The Engineer, 1874-1914*. New York and London, 1983.

NOWLAN, K.B., and WILLIAMS, T.D. *Ireland in the War Years and After*. Dublin, 1969.

O'CONNOR, Harvey. *The Guggenheims: The Making of an American Dynasty*. New York, 1937.

O'MAHONY, David. *The Irish Economy. An Introductory Description*. Cork, 1964.

ORCHARD, Harry. *Confessions and Autobiography of Harry Orchard* (Albert E. Horsley). New York, 1907.

PARKER, John. *Great Art Sales of the Century*, London, 1975.

PARSONS, A.B. *Porphyry Copper*. New York, 1933.

PETERSON, Richard H. *The Bonanza Kings: Social Origins and Business Behaviour of Western Mining Entrepreneurs, 1870-1900*. Lincoln, Nebraska, 1977.

PRAIN, Sir Ronald. *Copper. The Anatomy of an Industry.* London, 1975.

———. *Reflections on an Era: Fifty Years of Mining in Changing Africa.* London, 1981.

RÉAMONN, Seán. *History of the Revenue Commissioners.* Dublin, 1981.

REITLINGER, Gerald. *The Economics of Taste.* 3 Vols. London, 1961, 1963 and 1970.

RICKARD, Thomas Arthur. *A History of American Mining.* New York, 1932.

———. *Interviews with Mining Engineers.* San Francisco, 1922.

ROBINSON, Howard W. *Irish Statute Law relating to Income Tax, Sur-Tax and Corporation Profits Tax.* Dublin, 1953.

SAARINEN, Aline B. *The Proud Possessors.* New York, 1958.

SIRINGO, Charles A. *A Texas Cowboy, or, Fifteen Years on the Hurricane Deck of a Spanish Cow Pony.* New York, 1886.

———. *The Cowboy Detective.* New York, 1912.

TAYLOR, Francis Henry. *Pierpont Morgan.* New York, 1957.

THOMAS, Alan G. *Great Books and Great Collectors.* London, 1975.

TOWNER, Wesley. *The Elegant Auctioneers.* New York, 1970.

TRACY, Honor. *Mind You, I've Said Nothing! Forays in the Irish Republic.* London, 1953.

———. *The Straight and Narrow Path.* London, 1956.

WALL, Mervyn. *Leaves for the Burning.* London, 1952.

WATSON, Sir Malcolm. *African Highway. The Battle for Health in Central Africa.* London, 1953.

WHITE, Terence de Vere. *Big Fleas and Little Fleas, and other Stories.* London, 1976.

WILSON, Arthur J. *The Pick and The Pen. A History of Mining Journalism.* London, 1979.

WILSON, Arthur J. *The Life and Times of Sir Alfred Chester Beatty.* London, 1985.

WINGFIELD, Shiela (Lady Powerscourt). *Sun Too Fast*. London, 1974.

WYMAN, Mark. *Hard Rock Epic. Western Miners and the Industrial Revolution 1860-1910*. Los Angeles, California, 1979.

(d) *Articles and Pamphlets*

ARNOLD, Bruce, 'The Chester Beatty Library'. *Cara Magazine*, Vol. 2, No. 4, Oct./Dec. 1969.

BODMER, Daniel. Speech delivered at the opening of the Martin Bodmer Foundation on 15 June 1972. *Librarium* (Review of the Society of Swiss Book Collectors), Vol. 15, No. 2, Aug. 1972.

BODMER, Martin. 'Bibliotheca Bodmeriana'. *The Book Collector*. London, 1958.

British Bulletin of Commerce (War-Time Trading Bulletin). No. 109. 'The United Kingdom Commercial Corporation Survey 1940-44'.

British Museum Society Bulletin. No. 33, March 1980. 'Sir John Forsdyke and Sir Thomas Kendrick'.

CHAPMAN, Jan. 'Dublin's Gallery of Oriental Art'. *Far East Magazine*, Sept./Oct. 1975.

———. 'Ireland's Treasure House of Oriental Art'. *Okura Lantern Magazine*, Vol. 17, No. 1, Spring 1959.

DOYLE, David. 'The Irish and American Labour, 1880-1920'. *Saothar* (Journal of the Irish Labour History Society). Vol. I (1975).

Eire Ireland (Bulletin of the Department of External Affairs). 'Chester Beatty Paintings', No. 51: 11 Sept. 1950. 'Irish Bookbinding', No. 235: 24 May, 1954. 'Sir Alfred Chester Beatty', No. 774: 8 Feb. 1968.

GREEN, E.R.R. 'The Irish in American Business and Professions', in Doyle, David, & Edwards, Owen D. *America and Ireland 1776-1976*. Connecticut, 1980.

HAYES, Richard J. 'The Chester Beatty Library'. *The Book Collector*, London, 1958.

———. *The Chester Beatty Library, Dublin*. Dublin, 1958.

———. 'Sir A. Chester Beatty and his Library', *Princeton*

University Library Chronicle. Vol. XXVIII, No. 3, Spring 1967.

———. 'Die Chester Beatty Library in Dublin', *Librarium*, Vol. 16, No. 2, Aug. 1973.

HENCHY, Patrick. *The Chester Beatty Library, Dublin*. Dublin, 1982.

HENDERSON, Gordon. 'An Interview with Mervyn Wall'. *The Journal of Irish Literature*, Vol. XI, Jan./May 1982.

HOBSON, Dick. 'Dublin's imperishable memorial to a great philanthropist'. *Horizon* (Magazine of Rhodesian Selection Trust Limited), Oct. 1968.

HYNES, Malachy. 'The Orient in Dublin'. *The Pallotine*, Sept. 1968.

JAMES, David. 'Sir Alfred Chester Beatty and his Islamic Collection', in *Islamic Masterpieces of the Chester Beatty Library*. London, 1981.

———. 'The new Oriental Gallery at the Chester Beatty Library'. *Ireland Today*, No. 870, 13 Aug. 1975.

JESSOP, Norma and NUDDS, Christine J. *Guide to Collections in Dublin Libraries*. Dublin, 1982.

KELLY, F.M. 'The Chester Beatty MSS'. *Apollo*, Vol. XV, No. 89, May 1932.

KENNEDY, Brian P. 'Sir Chester Beatty: Friend and Patron of Ireland'. *Irish Times*, 7 Feb. 1985.

———. 'Sir Alfred Chester Beatty', *Ireland Today*, No. 1031, Sept. 1986.

———. 'Alfred Chester Beatty and the National Gallery of Ireland', *Irish Arts Review*, Vol. 4, No. 1, Spring 1987.

KENNEDY, Maev. 'The Chester Beatty'. *Irish Times*, 27 Jan. 1981.

KIDD, C.A. *Masons Avenue: The Story of Selection Trust Building*. London, 1985.

McCARTNEY, Donal. *The National University of Ireland and Eamon de Valera*. Dublin, 1983.

McHUGH, James N. 'The Chester Beatty Library and Gallery of Oriental Art'. *Ireland of the Welcomes*, Vol. 25, No. 6, 1976.

McPARLAND, Edward. 'A Dublin Treasure House'. *The*

Belvederian (Magazine of Belvedere College, Great Denmark Street, Dublin), Vol. XVIII, No. 1, 1958.

MacGOWAN, Gerard. 'The Chester Beatty Collection'. *Irish Tatler and Sketch*. Sept. 1954.

MALKIN, Solomon M. 'Beatty at Princeton'. *Antiquarian Bookman*, 20 Mar. 1967.

MONTGOMERY, David. 'The Irish and the American Labor Movement' in Doyle, David & Edwards, Owen D. *America and Ireland 1776-1976*. Connecticut, 1980.

MUNBY, A.N.L. 'Sir Thomas Phillipps: a Centenary Tribute'. *Art at Auction*, 1971-72. London, 1972.

O'CALLAGHAN, Margaret. 'Language, Nationality and Cultural Identity in the Irish Free State 1922-7: The *Irish Statesman* and the *Catholic Bulletin* reappraised'. *Irish Historical Studies*, Vol. XXIV, No. 84, Nov. 1984.

PEARSON, J.D. *Oriental Manuscript Collections in the Libraries of Great Britain and Ireland*. London, 1954.

RAU, Arthur. 'Bibliotheca Bodmeriana. Part I: Manuscripts'. *The Book Collector*. London, 1958.

———. 'Bibliotheca Bodmeriana. Part II: Printed Books'. *The Book Collector*. London, 1959.

USHIODA, Yoshiko. 'Sir Alfred Chester Beatty and Japan', in Sorimachi, Shigeo *Illustrated Books and Manuscripts in the Chester Beatty Library*. Tokyo, 1979.

WATSON, R.J.B. 'Collecting Works of Art'. *Burlington Magazine*, Vol. 107, Jan./June 1965.

WILKINSON, J.V.S. 'The Chester Beatty Library', *An Leabharlann*. Vol. 14, 1956.

———. 'The Chester Beatty Library'. *Ireland of the Welcomes*, Vol. 5, No. 6, Mar./Apr. 1957.

WITT, Sir Robert. *The Art of Collecting*. London, 1950.

Index